PETROGLYPHS
ANCIENT LANGUAGE / SACRED ART

PETROGLYPHS
ANCIENT LANGUAGE/SACRED ART

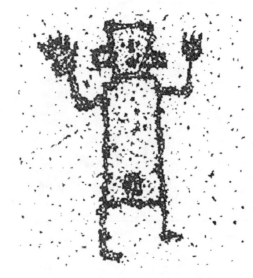

TEXT AND DRAWINGS BY
SABRA MOORE

CLEAR LIGHT PUBLISHERS
SANTA FE, NEW MEXICO

Copyright © 1998 Sabra Moore.

Clear Light Publishers, 823 Don Diego, Santa Fe, N.M. 87501
WEB: www.clearlightbooks.com

First Edition
10 9 8 7 6 5 4 3 2 1

Library of Congress Cataloging-in-Publication Data
Moore, Sabra.
    Petroglyphs: ancient language, sacred art / Sabra Moore.
        p. cm.
    ISBN: 1-57416-011-7 (cloth)
    1. Indians of North America—Antiquities.   2. Petroglyphs—North America.
    3. Rock paintings—North America.   4. North America—Antiquities.   I. Title.
    E98.P34M66 1998
    970.01—dc21
                                                                    98–11903
                                                                    CIP

FRONTISPIECE: *This thousand-year-old masked figure was uncovered in 1969 when a bulldozer cleared a private road near Nanaimo City, Vancouver, revealing a rock field of over thirty animated images incised into the surface, many wearing bird faces. Their age was estimated by the depth of forest soil that had preserved them.*

DRAWING (ABOVE): *The metal disk incised with an open hand may have been used as a paint palette by a Hopewell artist. This Ohio culture dates from 100 B.C. to A.D. 600.*

CONTENTS

FOREWORD

This is a rare book on petroglyphs and pictographs—not scholarly but informed, written with respect but not off-the-wall romanticism. It is, of course, off-the-wall in another sense. Rock art is literally and figuratively rooted in place. Each image is part of a much larger whole that may include one sacred site, miles of canyon, the length of a river, or vast borderless territories. Long an enthusiastic seeker of local southwestern sites, Sabra Moore has also browsed in books on places she hasn't been, singling out the images that moved her most. Her brief texts are informal, informative but never definitive, and frankly speculative, full of questions for herself and the reader. The issues raised may be as quotidian as her dog being uneasy at the sound of a Brazilian rainstick (which led Moore to understand another level of the affinities between snakes and rain in rock art, ominous music added to sinuous line and movement). Or they may reflect her anxiety about what is happening to the natural forces summoned by Native believers. Or they may recall a childhood experience.

      This is an art book rather than a textbook. Moore's beautiful drawings are as faithful to the originals as most photographs can be, echoing in their fidelity some of the pre-photographic historical records. In the process of translating the glyphs from stone to paper, an indirect collaboration has taken place between the ancient artist and the modern artist. The result lies tantalizingly between knowledge and ignorance, marking a fragile bond across time and cultures. Moore's own art—multilayered xeroxed books, almost abstract sculptures and installations dense with color and detail—bear no outward resemblance to this project, but time and human connections are their subject too; the hand and heart are familiar.

      As Moore says, her book is like an exhibition curated by an artist. It is a western rather than a Native notion, such a collection, uprooted as it is to be brought together in another medium. At the same time, she has included an image that lies in the arroyo below her Abiquiu home, an image we have visited together, not closing the circle, but continuing the spiral.

LUCY R. LIPPARD

PROTECTING
PETROGLYPHS

In continuing to uphold our past traditions and religion that are embodied in the petroglyphs, we still use certain areas for sacred ceremonies that have been going on for centuries before the time of the Spanish Conquistadors and the White Man, and certain of our societies and clans regularly visit these sites or shrines in the way of our ancestors.

To us these petroglyphs are not the remnants of some long lost civilization that has been dead for many years . . . they are part of our living culture. What is stored in the petroglyphs is not written in any book or to be found in any library. We need to return to them to remind us of who we are and where we came from, and to teach our own sons and daughters of it.

The petroglyphs are under a severe threat from vandalism and land development activities. For this reason, there is a need to protect the petroglyphs in a way that will allow us to continue to use them for religious purposes, as well as to save them for the benefit of both Indians and non-Indian visitors who come to appreciate our culture.

HERMAN AGOYO, San Juan Pueblo
All Indian Pueblo Council Chairman (1986–1990)
Statement before the U.S. House of Representatives Committee on Interior and Insular Affairs, Albuquerque, New Mexico, October 11, 1988

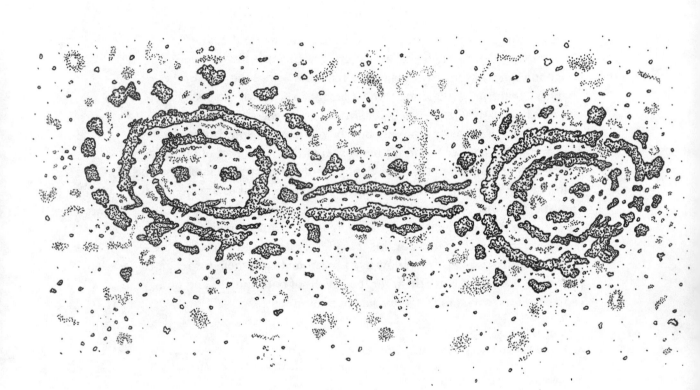

DRAWING PETROGLYPHS

I camped and hiked in the Southwest for many years before moving to New Mexico to live on a clear mesa in Abiquiu. The first pictograph I remember seeing was an ancient hand printed on a rock face in Bandelier National Monument. It was made by pressing a red pigmented palm onto a cave wall. Nearby were petroglyphs, incised images pecked into rock. I began drawing petroglyphs and pictographs in my journal, standing in the sun or balanced against a rock, drawing in ink as a way of really seeing the image. Some of the images are startling; the drawing conventions vary widely from region to region—differing treatments of scale and emphasis render a figure or animal natural or supernatural.

Once I was in Mexico, at the temples in Chichen Itza, drawing as other tourists passed, snapping photos and moving on. Someone asked me, "Are you an archaeologist?" "No, I'm an artist." A pause to digest this puzzle. But really, I was working within the long history of art. The idea of drawing as a way to learn was the dominant method before the invention of the

The conjoined circles on the left page are incised among other celestial images into a two-acre limestone "field" overlooking the Pecos River near Lewis Canyon, Texas— an area occupied continuously for 9,000 years. The circles mirror the sky. Further north in New Mexico, a Pueblo observer might consider this image an eccentric rendering of the traditional sun symbol—three concentric circles. Here, everything is doubled and a ring of dots circles each "sun."

camera and the proliferation of printed images. During the Renaissance in Europe and Asia, artists learned their craft by "copying" the masters or looking at engravings. We live in a century of "copies," but we think we're looking at the "real" thing. Our experience of world art today is based on photo reproductions in books, magazines, or postcards. But a photo is a frame. We are still seeing through a second artist's eye, but with the illusion of "being there."

Drawing is a physical process. Your eyes have to follow the image along the line, in this instance a pecked line that varies with the tool and quality of rock. Like making the original, it takes time; you don't see the whole until you are finished. Of course, I haven't left the camera entirely. Though some drawings are from "life," most are redrawn from photographs.

This book is a collection of images drawn from all regions of the country. It is not a survey; the subject is too vast. I have chosen the petroglyphs as I would pictures for an exhibit, based on their beauty, complexity, and meaning. I invite the reader to "look closely" with me.

The intricately pecked mask on the right has vanished under the lake in the Glen Canyon region of Utah, created by damming the Colorado River. It probably dates from the twelfth or thirteenth century, a period of elaborate design in Anasazi art. The maze pattern is continuous. I drew it starting at the broken line in the center of the mask. If it were a thread it could be unraveled. The stylized stepped clouds above the maze evoke rain, but not the calculated flood that engulfed this image.

THE VISIBLE LANGUAGE OF PETROGLYPHS

Petroglyphs are everywhere on this continent. They are the root of our art history and the visible root of our cultural history. Some are very ancient and some recent. This art was pecked into remote rock faces or above stone shelters, inside caves or ceremonial rooms, or alongside watering places, near animal trails, food gathering spots, or sites for cultivation. Some of these spaces were used over time and embellished by successive generations, as cathedrals, museums, and temples have been used, the imagery reinterpreted to fit changing needs.

The creators of this monumental art were from the 500 Indian nations inhabiting this continent for the past 30,000 years. Their descendants are here today.

Some sites remain active religious centers for contemporary Native peoples. All sites are sources of inspiration. Petroglyphs are literally embedded in the landscape. Their location is part of their meaning. It takes time to see rock art. It requires a certain slant of light and shadow for the image to be visible. Getting there can be a pilgrimage.

This book is an idiosyncratic travel guide to this vast outdoor museum. Some of the artworks shown here can't be visited. They are gone, destroyed by vandals, dam building, or careless roadwork. Others have been harmed by admiration. Chalking or rubbing can damage the drawings. Visit the petroglyphs lightly.

This figure from Bighorn Basin, Wyoming, was pecked in silhouette like an inverse sculpture. It was made between the fourteenth and eighteenth centuries. The artist may have been Shoshone. You don't see facial features; the head-dress defines the man. He seems to be wearing an old-style Plains "stand-up" feathered bonnet. His frontal stance indicates a personage, not a person, unlike the convention of later narrative art that recorded individual military exploits.

WHAT IS
PICTURE WRITING?

They are not only on rocks—images were incised into shell, chewed into bark, inscribed on trees, or painted and pecked on stone or animal hide. *Webster's Dictionary* defines "pictograph" as "a picture representing an idea" or "writing" and refers the reader to "hieroglyphic," "a symbol sign . . . hard to understand." People currently use "pictograph" to describe an image painted on rock. "Petroglyph" is simpler, defined as a "carving," "any inscription cut into the face of a cliff or a rock." The definition for "picture" is also straightforward, "an image or likeness of an object." As an action, "picture" means "to make visible" or "to show clearly." Why is picturing something "clear" but picture writing "hard to understand"? Are the pictographs a language, as the word implies? Many ethnologists have thought so. Colonel Garrick Mallery, writing a report for the Smithsonian in 1888, attempted to make sense of petroglyphs and pictographs as symbolic language. The year is no accident. The Battle of the Little Bighorn was in 1876, Geronimo surrendered in 1886, the massacre at Wounded Knee was 1890. Mallery was a military commander on the Missouri River whose interest was sparked by a Dakota Winter Count; by 1888, it was "safe" to look at the art but perhaps hard to talk with the people.

Some of that art can be considered writing. The Winter Counts, for instance, are Plains Indian calendars drawn on hide or cloth. Some contain drawings for 150 years or more. A "Keeper of the Count" would paint a single symbol each winter that could be "read" as the emblematic event of the year, thus composing a visual history for the tribe. The mnemonic images inscribed on Ojibwa birch bark scrolls are also "language"—songs and healing recipes that can be "read" by an initiate in the Midewiwin Society. Algonquian warriors carved records of military victories into trees. The Plains people had complex symbols for military honors. A hand for instance, symbolized "counting coup" on an enemy, and horse tracks, the route of horse capture. Painted on clothing or robes, these symbols recounted a personal history of achievement visible to all. They could be compared to the heraldic devices of Medieval Europe.

But do the diverse images of animals, people in various dress and gestures, elaborate headdresses, supernaturals, composite creatures, abstract patterns, hands, eyes, stars, suns, plants—make up a "picture language"? Every culture has visual conventions. All art is "clear" when you know the story. Look at Christian art. Everyone knows the story—the lamb is Christ; the crucifix, the cross, the tree. You can enjoy the formal qualities in the paintings because the story is implicit. When Europeans brought the cross to the Southwest, the Native people naturally interpreted this symbol as the four sacred directions or as a rather rigid rendering of the Morning Star. Is the cross "picture writing"? Are we sometimes unable to see the petroglyphs "clearly" as art because the story is unclear?

The inscribed stone below was found on the beach at Glen Cove, Long Island, in 1921 and donated to the extraordinary collection of Native American art housed at the Museum of Natural History in New York, alongside the dioramas of stuffed animals and the great dinosaur bones. It is catalogued as "possible example of picture writing."

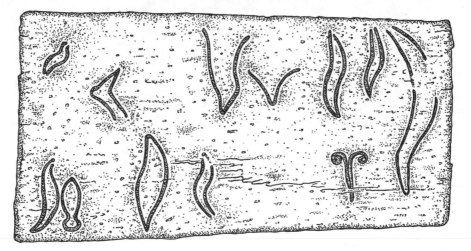

8

SOUTHWEST

Zuni. Hopi. Chiricahua Apache. Pueblos speaking Tewa, Keres, Towa, and Tiwa. Navajo. Lipan Apache. Comanche. Tohono O'Odham. Mescalero Apache. Pima. Havasupai.

These are the people whose ancestors punctuated the mesas, mountains, deserts, and riverways of the Southwest with outdoor galleries of rock art.

The person in the drawing on the left is planted firmly above the doorway of a cave room in Puyé Cliff, New Mexico, an Anasazi village inhabited from the fourteenth to eighteenth centuries. These ruins are maintained by neighboring Santa Clara Pueblo. The word for their kin was bestowed by outsiders—*Anasazi* is Navajo for "ancient people." *Puyé* is a Tewa word, however; it means "cottontail rabbit place." The rabbits are still there.

The man is in ceremonial dress with three feathers on his head. The doorway has a human shape. The village of Puyé stands on a mesa top and these cave rooms are on the cliff face just below. The caves are natural, but they have been altered by carving into the pink and white pumice rock. Some have simply been enlarged into back rooms of stone and adobe houses, but other rooms may be ceremonial. The doorways vary. This one is a body mold you can just fit through. The open sky and wooded valley are framed by the door shape. Some caves have holes carved at upper angles through the walls, suggestive of star viewing. Why is the man there? He seems to be singing or speaking. He faces the sky too.

We are still in New Mexico, with more figures raising their arms. This is a vulnerable gesture. In the movies, it signifies surrender, giving yourself up. Here is a different category of surrender—a kind of prayer.

This woman floats on a smoke-darkened cave ceiling at Otowi, a village contemporary with Puyé. You have to lie down in the small room to see her; your position is vulnerable as well. Her room is adjacent to another picture cave with viewing holes connecting the two rooms. Four erotic flute players and many spotted animals embellish the walls and ceiling. The woman could be Mother of the Animals, a Pueblo deity of many guises. Her womb is drawn in thick outline. She gave birth to the game animals—deer, antelope, rabbit, elk, mountain sheep; she controls fertility and the right of the people to hunt. Food is sacred; like women, food gives life. Taos Pueblo reveres the Deer Mother; many Pueblos, the Corn Mother. Does the image drawn on a cave ceiling suggest her position in the night sky? Or should we view the cave itself as an ornamented sculpture?

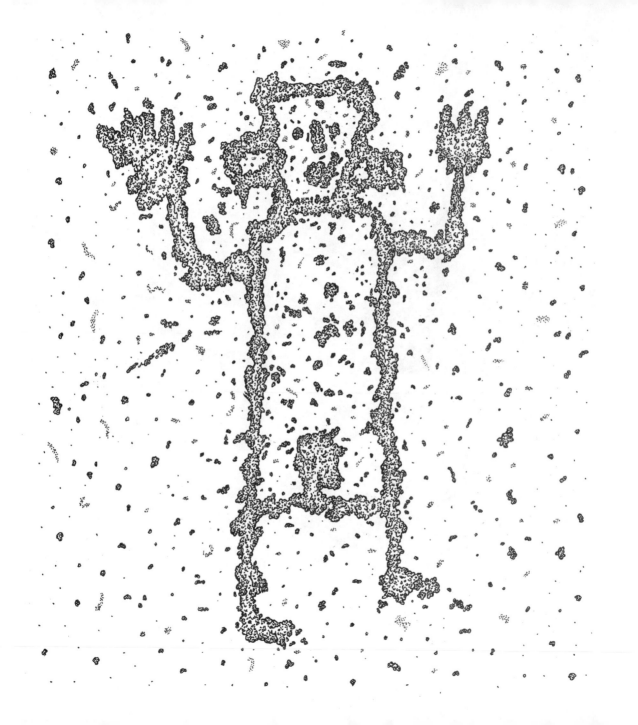

Traveling up the Rio Grande past Santa Clara and San Juan Pueblos, we are now away from the towns. The river has created a vast canyon littered with basalt boulders improbably balanced along its slopes. In the canyon are miles and miles of petroglyphs—individual figures, perhaps a bird or a man with a shield. You stop the car and get out to climb the slope. The artists have considered every possibility of rock position—some rocks drawn on like an elaborately tattooed arm, the images revealed as you circle, climb, look back, look up. This is a kinetic site; you move and the drawings shift.

What are the artists' purposes? Who are the intended viewers? The river? birds? people? Is this place an offering? Once my companion and I found two rocks that seemed to be directional markers. We followed both and found a clearly outlined rectangle similar to the one pecked on the rock. Is this enclosure for ritual purposes? We were trespassing, of course. These boulders are on private land, protected only by the goodwill of the landowners and the power of the art.

The images on the rocks include ducks, pregnant women, sun shields, spirals, turkeys, mountain lions, snakes, flute players, ants, masks, lizards, horned toads, banners, birds. Most date from the fourteenth to seventeenth centuries, but some could be 5,000 years old. Here is a person with upraised arms—the clothing suggests a woman. She wears horns, a symbol of spiritual power; her hands seem to be blurred with motion. I can't identify her animal companions. They resemble vastly enlarged kangaroo mice. These tiny mice bounce and hop; you often see them after rain. Or they could be long-eared coyotes.

The artists worked with several kinds of tools: sharp or blunt hammerstones, chiseled rocks, earth pigments. Some images are pecked, some scored, others are painted softly in red. They selected the sites, often choosing walls naturally "varnished" with dark pigments or cave ceilings purposefully blackened with smoke. Pecking uncovers the lighter surface and optically reverses the etching. In place of shadow, you see line. Like the Surrealists, the petroglyph artists took advantage of accident, amplifying a natural stripe or an evocative rock form. Unlike the Surrealists, their visual play was rooted in content. These artists weren't trying to startle. They were working with a shared visual language.

It is a complex language. Some southwestern rock art dates from 1000 B.C.; other images were made by Pueblo shepherds late in the nineteenth century. Many rock art panels contain images from several periods, the earlier art attracting new drawings. How can you "read" these images? Scholars are trying to chart the visual iconography by assembling lists of styles and figures. We don't try to "read" the language of European art starting with the caves at Lascaux through the paintings of Matisse. Southwestern rock art has an equally long history of development.

Rock art is literally embedded in its site. It can't be carried home in a shopping bag, unlike the devalued art of industrial societies. And it has a theatrical aspect: light and the time of day reveal or conceal the images.

This buffalo dancer faces a man in European-style hat and boots, visual evidence of the probable eighteenth-century dating of the red pictograph. An Apache artist might have painted the dancers along the cliff walls at Devil's River, near the Texas/Mexico border, an area dubbed *despoblado* by Spanish colonists, ignoring the 10,000 years habitation of this "unpopulated zone." A succession of artists from early hunter-gatherers to Cibola, Jumano, Apache, Comanche, Kiowa, and Kickapoo left abundant testimony of their presence on the canyon and cliff walls.

This Galisteo, New Mexico, petroglyph can be roughly dated after the fourteenth century. It is a masked kachina topped by an ascending bird—both messengers of rain. Kachinas visit pueblos early each year in the form of dancers dressed like this figure. They are relatively "new," introduced into the Southwest in the fourteenth century, possibly through trade with Mexico.

The Galisteo Basin is an ancient riverbed, now an expanse of rolling land south of Santa Fe dotted with ridges of jagged upright boulders. These "hogbacks" are covered with rock art created by people from Galisteo and Pecos Pueblos or their Anasazi ancestors. The surfaces are flat and striated with cracks. Their towns were abandoned in the nineteenth century; the ruins are now privately owned. This place was a crossroads between Plains and Pueblo people, a site of trade, conflict, and cultural exchange. This is still true of contemporary Galisteo, home to artists, ranchers, and Hispanic villagers.

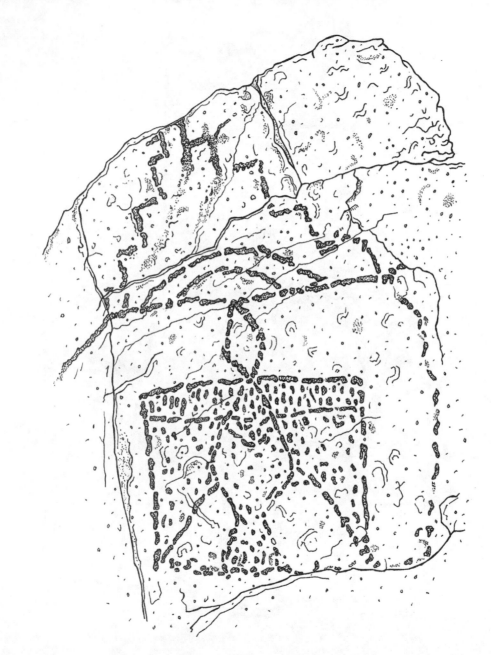

A Desert Mogollon artist, southern "cousin" to the Anasazi, pecked this bird near the edge of a rock face at Three Rivers, New Mexico. This site contains over 500 rock drawings made between the eleventh and fifteenth centuries. The bird is flying to both actual and symbolic clouds with prayers for rain—the cloud terrace at its beak is also an altar.

Scholars have divided the Indians of the Southwest prior to the fifteenth century into three major cultures: Anasazi, Hohokam, and Mogollon. The Fremont were their Great Basin neighbors in Utah. All are ancestors of contemporary Pueblo Indians. We don't know their original names. *Hohokam* is a Pima word meaning "those who have gone"; Mogollon was an early Spanish governor of New Mexico. The Fremont were named after the Fremont River in south-central Utah where many ancient farms were located. The river was named for John Charles Frémont, "The Pathfinder," who explored routes across Oregon, Idaho, Utah, and Nevada to the west coast. The paths he found led through other peoples' lands; the wagon and rail routes were a locus for trade for European settlers, resistance and disease for Indians. Frémont was helped across Utah by Truckee, a Paiute guide who, of course, knew the routes through his native country. The bird in the drawing is a pathfinder of a different nature.

You often find snakes pecked into rocks near springs or above rivers. The ones with horns could be associated with Quetzalcoatl, the Feathered Serpent of the Aztec pantheon. Sometimes they have crosses on their tails in a combination snake/star. Some have one horn, some two. In New Mexico, a double-horned snake may be the sacred Avanyu. A single-horned water serpent in Arizona could be the Hopi Paalölöqangw or at Zuni, Kolowisi.

Some snakes are simply rattlesnakes, like the ones drawn here. These are from White Rock Canyon near Los Alamos. They are a common desert animal. My spotted cattle dog found one coiled under a juniper next to the house, and warned me with her bark. One Christmas, I bought a rain stick from Brazil as a gift, a musical rattle made from hollowed bamboo. When we unwrapped it, we turned it back and forth to enjoy the trickling melody. My dog looked worried and wouldn't approach the stick. Her unease taught me a little about the rattlesnake as a symbol for rain. You hear the gourd rattle mingled with the bells on the corn dancers' legs during the summer ceremonials of the Pueblos. The sound mimics the rain we long for during those hot months.

On the following pages are two versions of horned snakes. The drawing on page 22 is a star/snake petroglyph near the abandoned pueblo of San Cristobal in the Galisteo Basin of New Mexico. On page 23 is an eight-foot horned serpent painted by a Mogollon artist around 500 B.C. near the present Diablo Dam in West Texas. The snake is painted in white over the soot-blackened ceiling of a huge cave. The stepped pattern inside its body may symbolize the flat-bottomed clouds that line southwestern horizons during rainy summers.

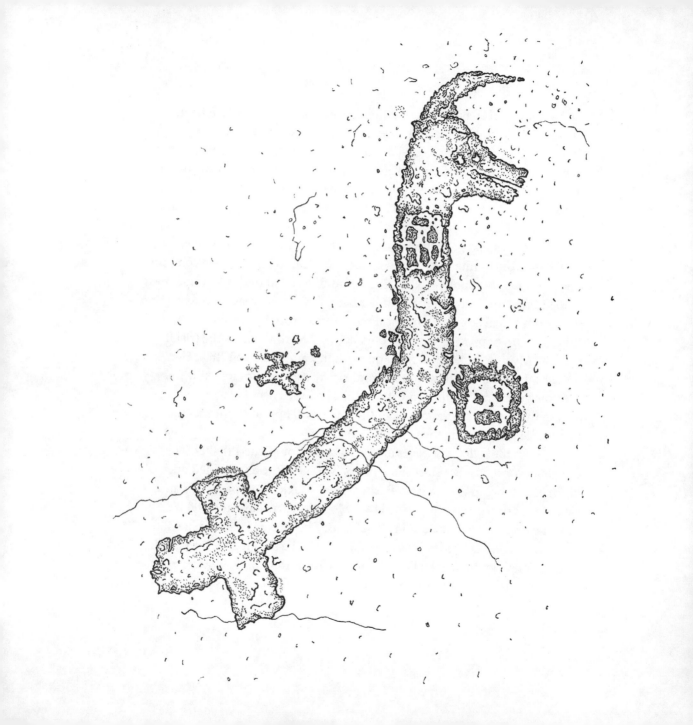

23

The Navajos call it "tank rain"—violent summer thunderstorms that can fill a metal water tank. I experienced one recently. Sitting outside at night after a drought-breaking rain, I heard a strange grinding sound, like a truck stuck in the canyon below. It was dark. We took the flashlight and climbed down the slope to see if someone needed help. No truck, nothing, just the whirring noise. My companion glanced north toward a temporary pond created by a neighbor's bulldozed road. Frogs, loudly celebrating in their watery haven! These tiny frogs live underground during dry periods and surface briefly inside ephemeral water holes.

These masks were painted in red on rock shelter walls at Hueco Tanks, a pre-industrial "tank rain" site near El Paso, home to Desert Mogollon cultures in the current border areas of Texas, New Mexico, and Chihuahua. They were "cousins" to the Mimbres, painters of the famous pottery, and worked at Hueco Tanks in the eleventh to fifteenth centuries, leaving many paintings of masks inside the natural shelters. *Hueco* is Spanish for "hollows"—this area is dotted with natural stone hollows or "tanks" that fill temporarily with water. Many of the masks are water gods, including some that represent the Mexican rain gods Tlaloc and Quetzalcoatl. The two masks in the drawing have watery attributes—a fish-shaped mouth on one and cloud terraces in the eyes of the other. The conical hats may be horns like the ones on sacred snakes.

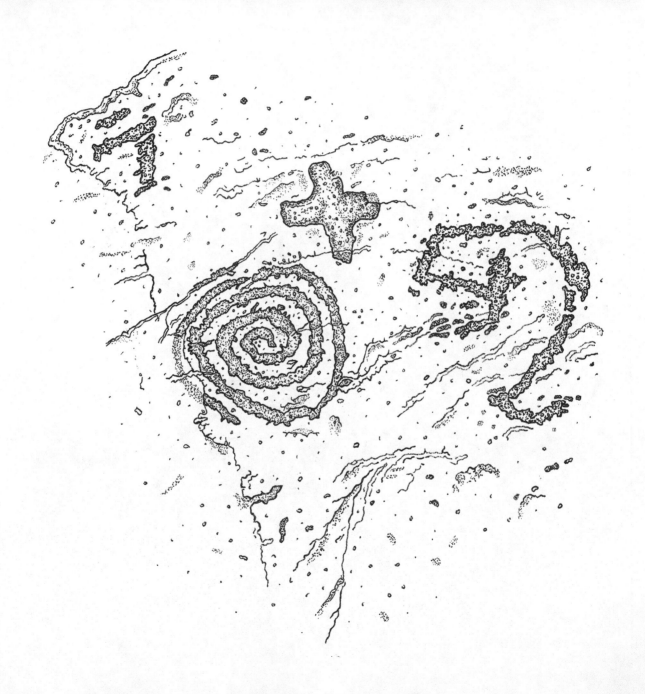

This spiral spins across a white cliff face near Abiquiu, New Mexico, flanked by the soft-pointed cross (the planet Venus) and a grouping of ambiguous petroglyphs. The helmet-shaped image on the right could be a star trail. Spirals may represent water or wind. Images of Venus appeared throughout ancient North America. The Mayas accurately computed her movements for many thousands of years. Plains people depicted the Morning Star in the shape of a Maltese cross, often painted red to symbolize sun power. The Chumash associated the Morning Star with rain but the Evening Star was the voracious chief of the underworld.

An Anasazi artist pecked this Venus across the canyon from a pictograph of Venus paired with the sun. I camped near here with a companion. Waking at dawn the day of the autumnal equinox, he spied the real Venus rising above its portrait. The remains of Anasazi gardens are on the mesas above these petroglyphs.

The Pueblo people are farmers whose ancestors developed calendars and star markers to aid in planting and harvesting. Growing food is sacred. Growing food in an arid climate requires acute attention and respect for natural forces. It is only recently that outsiders have noticed the abundant celestial markers, observatories, and sun shrines throughout the Southwest.

This rock drawing from Petrified Forest, Arizona, is probably a solstice marker. The shaded area on the upper left indicates where the sunlight bisects the sun-shaped image at midwinter, an observation first documented by artist Ann Preston and astronomer Robert Preston in 1985.

More star gazing appears on the next two pages. An eleventh-century Chacoan may have painted the pictograph on page 30 across the ceiling of a rock overhang below Peñasco Blanco in Chaco Canyon, New Mexico, mirroring the night sky overhead. Some astronomers believe it depicts the supernova that appeared near the crescent moon above Chaco on July 4, 1054. The two star beings on page 31 are part of a complex of Anasazi petroglyphs on the northwest side of rapidly expanding Albuquerque. Activists continue to fight to preserve Petroglyph National Monument and its rock art from destruction due to a proposed road through the lava escarpment.

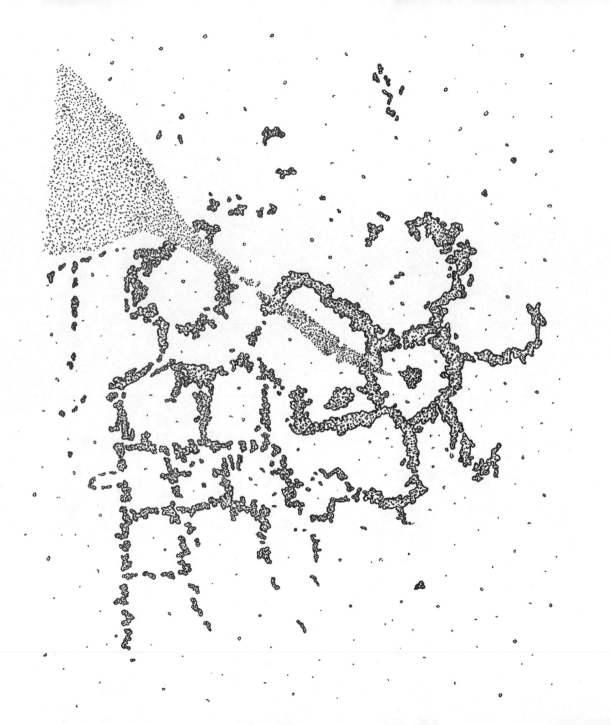

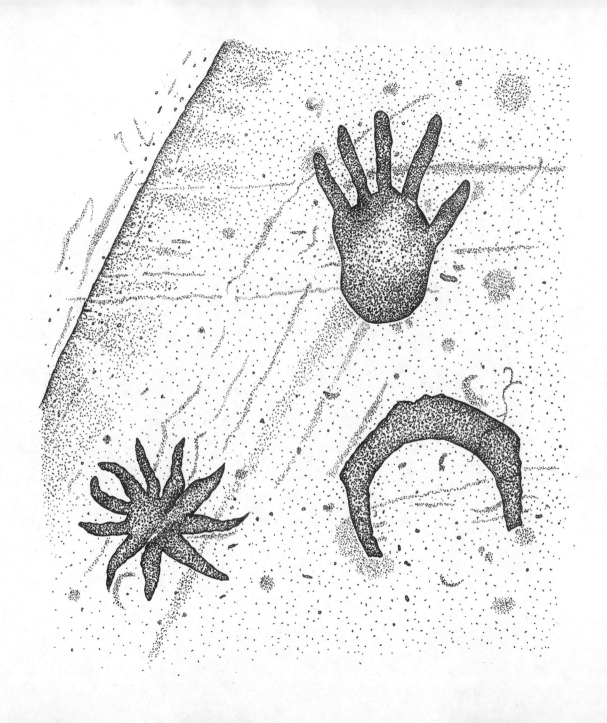

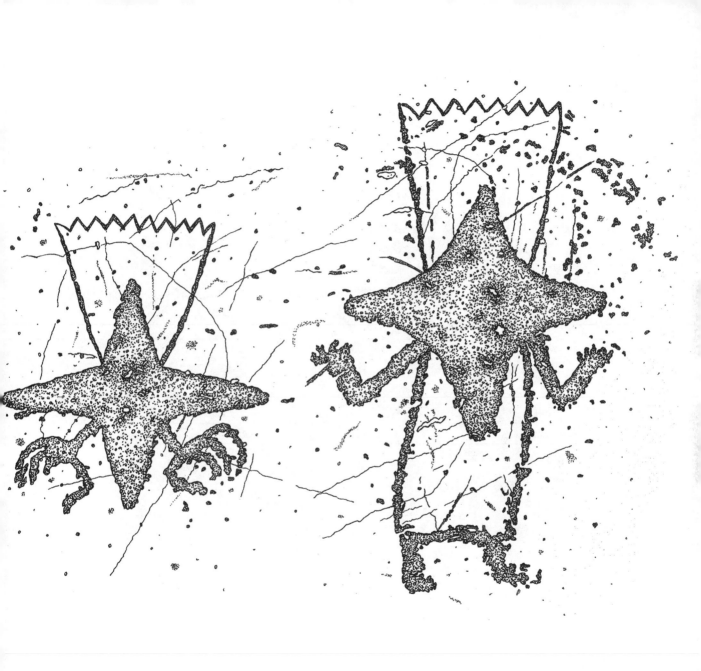

This eighteenth-century Navajo petroglyph depicts supernaturals associated with water and is suitably located along the Largo Canyon drainage of the San Juan River in New Mexico. The horned figure is *ghaan' ask' idii*, Humpback God. His feathery hump bulges with seeds and mists. He carries a staff and may be a guardian of mountain sheep. He is similar to the Pueblo flute-player, Kokopelli. Does this petroglyph signify journey? Humpback God's staff points to a pair of feet that seem about to enter a concentric maze.

The hourglass shape above the circle symbolizes another supernatural, Born-for-Water, one of the sacred War Twins. The hourglass is a stylized scalpknot. Born-for-Water helped his elder brother, Monster Slayer, kill some of the dangerous creatures that inhabited the nascent world. The older boy knocked the monsters down and the little brother scalped them. They are the children of the Sun and Changing Woman. Born-for-Water is considered the "parent of all waters."

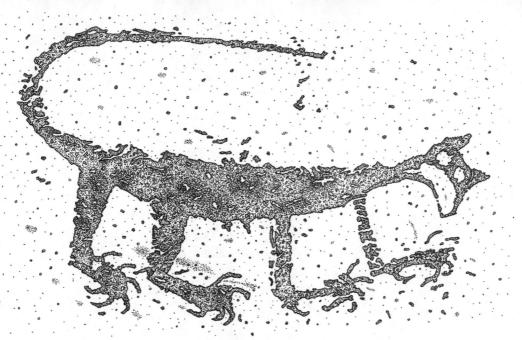

In the Pueblo origin stories, the first people climbed into our current world from a place underground. Tewa ethnologist Alfonso Ortiz locates this dark world "in Sipofene . . . far to the north" (Ortiz 1969, p. 13). People, animals, and the first mothers, Blue Corn Woman, the Summer mother, and White Corn Maiden, the Winter mother, lived together there. When it was time to emerge, the mothers asked a man to test the upper world. He tried, but the earth was "unripe." He climbed up again; the predatory mammals and scavenger birds were waiting in ambush. They attacked him, then pulled him up, restored him, and gave him the weapons and garb of a hunter. He returned underground as Mountain Lion and the Hunt Chief. This man divided the Tewa into Summer and Winter people, one group agricultural and the other hunting, the ceremonial division that still exists in contemporary Pueblo villages.

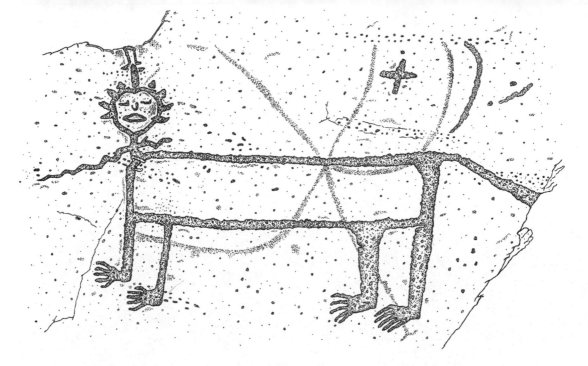

You can see Mountain Lion among the dancers of the winter Deer Dance in Taos Pueblo, portrayed by a boy. He points to the animals that the sacred clowns will "kill" with their tiny arrows.

The engraved mountain lion on the left dates after the fourteenth century. Her claws and tail spiral like the sun in a clockwise direction. This rock drawing is one of numerous wild cats depicted in Petrified Forest National Park, Arizona.

The composite animal above, incised on a boulder near the Rio Grande north of Española, New Mexico, has sky and earth symbolism— a sun face with a mountain lion body. Its feet resemble those of the bear, a powerful medicine animal. The snake bisecting its neck points toward a star; pecked scratch lines crossing the image could indicate a ritual function for this drawing.

In a traditional Zuni story, the Twin War Gods were concerned that humans were weak and the predator animals strong. They changed some animals into stone, creating powerful fetishes to protect people against negative forces. Nineteenth-century ethnologist Frank Cushing wrote, "And we often see among the rocks the forms of many beings that live no longer . . ." (Cushing 1883, pp. 14–15).

We also "see among the rocks" the animals that provide food for humans or lions, deer, and mountain sheep. The deer on the left is a spirit deer; the huge antlers indicate its spiritual power. It is on a panel of sheep and hunters created by Fremont artists between the tenth and twelfth centuries near Moab, Utah. The mountain sheep (right) could date from the sixth century. There are abundant rock drawings of sheep at Capitol Reef National Park, Utah, evidence of the sustenance they provided.

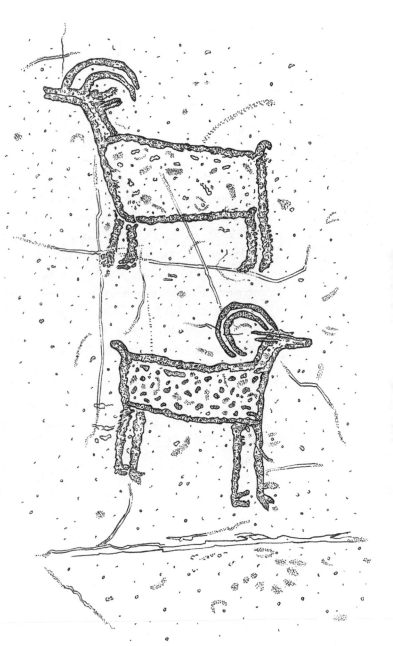

Depictions of Kokopelli, the humpbacked flute player on the right, can now be seen on dishes, jewelry, tee-shirts, and cards, usually without the phallus or antennae that characterize him on the cliffs and boulders where his image originates. Some Pueblo leaders warn against the commercialization of this sacred musician.

He appeared in the Southwest around the tenth century. Multiple Kokopellis can be seen all along the Rio Grande. This flute player is located near Velarde, New Mexico. Ethnolinguist Ekkehart Malotki traces his origin to the Hopi kachina Kookopölö. His erotic attire is both comic and sacred, intended to promote fertility among humans and plants. Kokopelli's flute was probably borrowed from the locust, a natural musician whose yearly emergence coincides with spring. At Hopi, the locust is a patron of the Flute Society.

This Kokopelli has assistance in calling the rain clouds from the mountains. The bird below his feet is ready to fly in the direction of a mountain sacred to neighboring San Juan Pueblo, possibly Chicoma to the west. The figure between them hides a concentric sun face behind a sun shield.

Not all Kokopellis are erotic, and not all erotic figures are Kokopellis. Some scholars of rock art think a lizard's tail can be seen as a phallus. This horned toad has stretched the tale, playing a prehistoric Rapunzel for the randy figure with a braid. Or is he an erotic ant with an antenna? The Anasazi artist selected the site with care, giving the figure a foothold at the edge of a cliff near Petrified Forest in Arizona.

PUBLIC SITES

Asterisk denotes a site discussed or illustrated in the previous sections.

The Southwest has been settled since the Clovis hunted the mammoth in 11,500 B.C. The land is layered with human presence. Be alert for rock art around places with water, spots where sacred mountains come into view, sites that cross animal trails, areas for piñon gathering, cliff shelters, unusual rock formations, sky-viewing spots or cliff sites near contemporary or ancient villages.

Here are a few public rock art locations to visit:

ARIZONA

Canyon de Chelly National Monument
Rock art made over a two-thousand-year period from various cultures, including Navajo and Basketmaker. Historic Navajo rock drawings can be seen in nearby Canyon del Muerto. Monument headquarters are in Chinle.

Casa Malpais
Mogollon site with several petroglyphs, located on Highway 60 in Springerville.

Glen Canyon National Recreation Area*
The rock art that has not been inundated by Lake Powell can be seen along the shoreline. The visitors' center is in Page.

Navajo National Monument
Two pristine Anasazi sites with pictographs by ancestors of contemporary Hopi. Take Route 160 from Tuba City to Route 564 and drive 9 miles to the visitors' center.

Newspaper Rock Petroglyphs, Petrified Forest National Park*
The images on this famous rock face one mile south of the Rio Puerco are among hundreds in the park. Petrified Forest is east of Holbrook between Interstate 40 and Highway 80.

Painted Rocks State Park
Many petroglyphs located west of Gila Bend. Drive 13 miles on Interstate 8, then 12 miles north on the marked access road.

COLORADO

Mesa Verde National Park
Beautiful cliff dwellings occupied for 800 years until around 1276. There are many petroglyphs, some on guided trails. Mesa Verde is 10 miles east of Cortez on Route 160.

NEW MEXICO

Bandelier National Monument*
A spectacular Anasazi site occupied for thousands of years until the fifteenth century. Petroglyphs and pictographs are visible along some of the cliff faces above the ruins and inside the cave rooms at both the excavated areas near the visitors' center and in the back country. Bandelier is on Route 4 near Los Alamos.

Carlsbad Caverns National Park

Pictographs at the cave entrance and at Painted Grotto near Slaughter Canyon. Take U.S. 62 south from Carlsbad, 18 miles to the park road.

Chaco Culture National Historic Park

Intricately crafted stone towns, over 2,000 sites in 32 square miles, petroglyphs, pictographs, solar "observatories," and a nexus of ancient roadways radiating outward, central to understanding the Indian Southwest. Chaco Canyon is located off Route 44 near Nageezi Trading Post amidst yellow canyons.

Petroglyph National Monument*

Rock art on basalt boulders along the Rio Grande pecked before the seventeenth century. The monument is located on the northwest side of Albuquerque off Interstate 40.

Puyé Cliff Ruins*

A small grouping of exquisite pink and yellow cliff dwellings built into the side of a mesa with rock drawings above the houses and along the cliff face. You can also climb to a ruin on the top of the mesa. The ruins are located on the Santa Clara Reservation off Route 30, 11 miles west of Española.

Three Rivers Petroglyph National Recreation Site*

More than 5,000 petroglyphs made by Mogollon artists between the tenth and fifteenth centuries. The site is located near Three Rivers off Highway 64.

TEXAS

Hueco Tanks State Historical Park*

Abundant pictographs and petroglyphs made by successive cultures attracted to the seasonal water in the natural hollows. They are located off Highway 62 at the intersection with Ranch Road 2775, 32 miles northeast of El Paso.

Seminole Canyon State Historical Park*

Many rock shelters, including Fate Bell Shelter, with over 200 pictograph sites dating back 4,000 years. Follow Highway 90, 9 miles west of Comstock, near the Pecos River High Bridge.

UTAH

Arches National Park

Numerous rock art sites among the dazzling formations, including Courthouse Wash Panel. The park headquarters at Moab can give directions for viewing petroglyphs.

Butler Wash Petroglyphs

Life-sized Anasazi rock drawings on a 200-yard-long panel visible by boat, 4 miles west of the town of Bluff on the San Juan River. Apply for permit at the Bureau of Land Management in Monticello.

Canyonlands National Park

Petroglyphs throughout spectacular rock formations. Canyonlands can be reached from Moab or Needles.

Capitol Reef National Park

Fremont era rock art visible from highway. The park is located 5 miles east of Torrey on Route 24.

Cave Canyon Towers

Seven stone towers near a cluster of petroglyphs with astronomical significance. Cave Canyon is near Blanding off Utah 95.

Clear Creek Canyon Rock Art
  Many rock drawings along Clear
  Creek, Mill Creek, and Dry Creek,
  between Sevier and Cove Fort
  on Utah 44.

Dinosaur National Monument
  Brontosaurus bones and Fremont
  rock art produced between the seventh
  and eleventh centuries. The visitors'
  center is on Route 149 off Highway
  40 at Jensen.

Dry Fork Canyon (McConkie Ranch)
  Fremont period rock art panels with
  human figures, located off Route 121
  about 3 miles north of Vernal.

Fremont Indian State Park*
  Over 12,000 Fremont rock drawings
  throughout the 900-acre park. The site
  is located on Interstate 70, 5 miles past
  Clear Creek Junction.

Grand Gulch Primitive Area
  Backpacking area with petroglyphs made
  over a thousand-year period. Drive to
  Kane Gulch on Utah 261, 4 miles
  south of Utah 95. A trail leads to
  Grand Gulch.

Horseshoe Canyon (Barrier Canyon)
  Many large pictographs of human
  figures. The site is accessible on a rough
  road from Hans Flat Ranger Station in
  Goblin Valley State Park.

*Little Black Mountain Petroglyph
Interpretive Site*
  Over 500 rock images from various
  cultures, 8 miles south of St. George. Road
  directions are available from the Bureau
  of Land Management in St. George.

Nine-Mile Canyon Rock Art
  Pictographs and petroglyphs made by
  Fremont artists before the thirteenth
  century are visible along the walls of Nine-
  Mile Canyon, located between
  Price and Myton on Utah 53.

Parowan Gap Indian Drawings
  Fremont rock drawings located on the
  county road off Interstate 15 at Parowan
  turnoff.

Sand Island Petroglyphs
  A large grouping of petroglyphs near the
  San Juan River. Drive 2 miles southwest
  from Bluff on U.S. 191.

Shay Canyon Petroglyphs
  Rock art on sandstone cliffs located 12
  miles west on Utah 211 off U.S. 191
  from Monticello.

Thompson Wash Petroglyphs
(also called *Sego Canyon*)
  Extensive rock carvings from three
  different cultures about 3 miles north of
  Thompson. Sego Canyon is marked on
  local road maps.

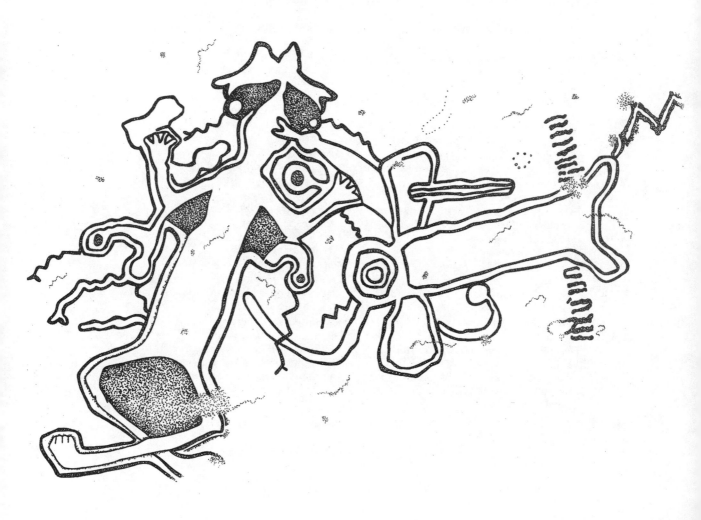

CALIFORNIA,
THE GREAT BASIN,
AND THE PLATEAU

I drew a detail of this one-hundred-foot Chumash wall painting from an 1894 photograph. The original in Carrizo Plains, California, can't be discerned through the pockmarks of bullets and rocks. The Chumash were the first people encountered on the California coast by Juan Rodriguez Cabrillo in 1542; he admired their spacious houses and elaborate hair styles. One of their two great provinces was ruled by an old woman, he said. By 1831, the 10,000 Chumash numbered slightly more than 3,000. Twenty contemporary Chumash families live on their reservation in California today.

The cave murals are often painted in four or more colors. Formally, these paintings resemble Russian Constructivist art, but the content and symbolism belie the comparison. I tried to find a break in the line, in excerpting this detail, but all the images are connected and flow into each other.

Campbell Grant documented Chumash cave paintings near Santa Barbara in the early 1960s. He is one of several distinguished artist-scholars who have revived interest in Native art. Artist Polly Schaafsma, the preeminent scholar of southwestern rock art, is another. Thirty years after Grant's research, we have a means to "read" some of the Chumash iconography. Scholars rediscovered eighty boxes of Chumash oral history collected after 1906 by Smithsonian anthropologist John Peabody Harrington and forgotten in storage at that institution.

The cave murals were painted by astronomer priests, perhaps under the visionary influence of datura. Most depict celestial events in a supernatural power struggle in which humans participate. The sun was a widower living in a quartz crystal house who carried a blazing torch as he crossed the sky. The moon was a woman who controlled human health and reproduction. Sky Coyote was the North Star, the humans' ally. Condor, Venus, Jupiter, and Saturn were deities. The supernaturals played a celestial ball game during the winter solstice: Sun versus Sky Coyote; Moon kept score. Things could go badly during this time, so the people held elaborate ceremonials to try to affect the game. There were ritual dances; priests worked with sun sticks; people erected great feathered poles and carried them to sun shrines.

The segmented circle in this painting from Painted Cave near San Marcos Pass in Santa Barbara is possibly the sun at home. The shapes on the right could be poles or banners.

There were over sixty Native cultures in California prior to European contact, including Pomo, Wappo, Miwok, Costanoan, Esselen, Chumash, Wintu, Patwin, Karok, Maidu, Yokut, Hupa, and Yurok. Scholars estimate the population was around 300,000 in 1769 and 20,000 in 1900. Native people did not profit from the Gold Rush.

People subsisted on the natural bounty of the region—salmon, oysters, shellfish, nuts, berries, small game. The climate is mild; you travel lightly. They made beautifully patterned carrying baskets, some worn as conical hats.

They ate seven varieties of acorns. Stones in the oak forests today are pocked with circular grinding pits where people ground acorns into flour. Pecked images are found near these sites. You also find rock drawings in the canyons and along the coast. Huge intaglio figures, some 175 feet long, dot the desert floor near Blythe. They are best viewed from the air.

Ukrainian artist Louis Choris visited the Spanish mission of San Francisco de Asis in 1816 and described a ceremonial dance he witnessed after church services: "Half the men adorn themselves with feathers and with bits of shell . . . or they paint their bodies with regular lines of black, red, and white. Some have half their bodies (from the head downward) daubed with black, the other half red, and the whole crossed with white lines. Others sift the down from birds on their hair . . ." (Trenton 1989, p. 163).

This Chumash painting near Santa Barbara may reflect more than the shaman's dream in its depiction of complex figures. The images could be sky deities. The splayed personage at the top might be an animal or a costume. This painting on a cave ceiling can be viewed in different sequences from the ground. The figures change when you reverse the images, moving between animal and insect attributes.

Traveling southeast near the California–Nevada border, you enter the Great Basin. Nothing flows to the ocean; the land contains desert, dry lake beds, mountains, and the dark basalt cliffs favored for rock drawing, formed by volcanos. The Northern Shoshone called this area *coso* or "fire"; their ancestors created over 20,000 drawings on the glossy rock walls and boulders. Since the 1940s, the Navy has owned the Coso Range. If you wish to visit, apply to the China Lake Naval Weapons Center. The art has to compete with missiles and rockets; the most active testing sites are among the petroglyph fields.

These ceremonial figures are pecked into the walls of Renegade Canyon and could date after 1000 B.C. These two stand as part of an elongated cluster of similar personages, each displaying a different style of sun face and patterned dress. The costumes have stripes, spirals, and checks. Their feet are bird feet. Each figure holds a stick in one hand and what might be arrows in the other. Campbell Grant helped survey this site in the 1960s. He called the sticks weapons—spear throwers or bow and arrows, in keeping with the military metaphor. They could as easily be fire-making tools, in keeping with their fiery faces. Or sacred thunderbolts like the ones hurled by Zeus. Or celestial digging sticks like those used by women to collect food.

This virile hunter has supernatural assistance in his pursuit of a bighorn sheep, his horned headdress attests to his spiritual power. The deep gorge of Sheep Canyon, aptly named by Campbell Grant, is a natural animal trap that was modified to conceal Coso Range hunters. It was a collaborative hunt, the bowmen waiting behind a rock blind while others stampeded the animals. They used weapons and art to capture the sheep. The walls are covered with almost 3,000 drawings; over half are portraits of sheep and many include hunters.

Is this "ritual magic," the act of drawing "calling" the sheep? Or does it reflect intense observation and identification with the animal that sustains people, an exchange in which the bighorn participates? Bering Sea traditional hunters to the north shared a similar experience with seals. In one story, a boy goes to live among bearded seals for a year. His animal host advises him about paying attention to his prey. "These then, when they start to go hunting/and use their eyes only for looking at their quarry/their eyes then are truly strong . . ." (Fitzhugh 1988, p. 262). This Shoshone hunter wears horns like his quarry, and his arm is one with the bow; his potency is obvious.

The Eastern Shoshone warrior on page 54 is painted realistically. The spirit lines across his red shield may have been drawn at a later period. Archaeologist Sally J. Cole dates this northwestern Colorado pictograph from the fourteenth to eighteenth centuries.

The drawing on page 55 is a detail from the famous petroglyph frieze at Newspaper Rock, Utah. A Ute ceremonial figure is shown dancing with a tiny buffalo and sheep. She looks like a cross-cultural cowgirl with fringed chaps and quirt, wearing a traditional spirit headdress. The Utes were pivotal in introducing horses captured from the Spanish into the Great Basin and Plains. Newspaper Rock is overlaid with 1,500 years of drawing, but the chaps and quirt place this image in the late nineteenth century.

Shoshone, Paiute, Ute, Bannock, Gosiute, Panamint, and other peoples have lived in the Great Basin since 10,000 B.C. Their neighbors settled the Columbia Plateau to the north a thousand years earlier, clustering along the river basins of the Columbia and Fraser Rivers that drain from the Rocky Mountains and the Cascades. The art of the Klickitat, Walla Walla, Palouse, Kutenai, Chilcotin, Carrier, Umatilla, Cayuse, Nez Perce, Coeur D'Alene, Flathead, Klamath, Modoc, Chinook, and Saknai adorns the rocks and cliffs bordering the rivers.

The rivers in central Idaho escaped the dam building that decimated rock art sites in other locations along the Columbia waterways. These standing figures are incised into a basalt boulder along Snake River near Buffalo Eddy, south of Lewiston, Idaho, their legs spread in a gesture of action typical of Columbia Plateau visual convention. They were probably made before the tenth century. The people vary in size, perhaps relating to importance or distance. Their arms are upraised and they seem to be dancing. Their stance resembles southwestern figures, but something is different; the fingers and toes are missing and the limbs simply rounded. Plains artists have a similar convention. They eliminate hands in Winter Count drawings, ending the wrist with a straight line.

The raised double "paddle" held aloft by the upper figure is peculiar to Buffalo Eddy drawings. Scholar James D. Keyser calls it a "barbell" and speculates that the person is a hunt-chief shaman. He stands adjacent to a ceremonial being with closely set horns or pincers and double loops for hands. Could this shape be a dance rattle? Or a boat paddle? Far south, overlooking the Pecos River in Crockett County, Texas, similar shapes appear, double circles connected by parallel lines, pecked across a "field" of sun and star drawings. Those are celestial images; these resemble eyes. Is some kind of spiritual vision being evoked here? And what of the modern barbell—simply a tool of the gym or symbol for physical prowess? Survival of early people depended on the physical intelligence of their bodies. Our worship of fitness has transcended mere health.

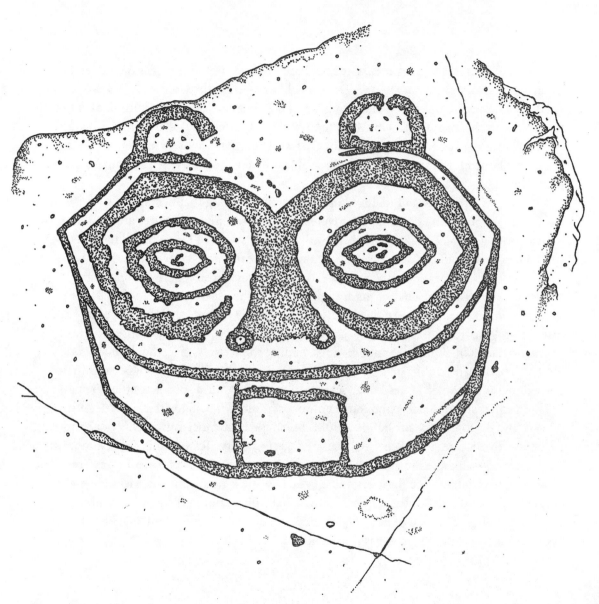

You can visit this nineteenth-century petroglyph, near the Dalles along the Columbia River in Horsethief Lake State Park, Washington. The word is derived from *dalle,* Old French for "gutter" or "drain," a prosaic origin for the dramatic cliffs that channel the Columbia River. The Dalles was the site of trade fairs between Columbia Plateau and Pacific Coast tribes; the French trappers who coined its name were late-comers to a long tradition of exchange. Lewis and Clark visited in 1806 and noted items found at the fair: "British or American muskets, powder, ball and shot, copper and brass kettles, brass tea-kettles . . . blankets . . . scarlet and blue cloth . . ." (Lewis and Clark 1893, Vol. III, p. 787). The middlemen and hosts were Wishram and Wasco people. Archaeologists dated this rock drawing by its association with similar trade items in Wishram cremation sites.

The figure is called Tsagiglalal, a Wishram name meaning "She Who Watches," and she watches over a cemetery. A Wishram woman shaman explained her expression, "People grin like that when they're sick . . . when people look at you like that, you get sick" (Keyser 1992, p. 101). Many Wishram sickened and died from the other form of goods brought by Europeans—smallpox, measles, whooping cough, tuberculosis, and diphtheria. By 1840, the Dalles had lost 90 percent of its Native population.

There are many images of Tsagiglalal, outdoor rock drawings and visages pecked on small stones and bones. Although she mirrors the face of death, Tsagiglalal was used as a guardian spirit in curing. Maybe the image of death could deflect death.

On the following page is a stone fragment rescued from an incised boulder flooded by the Dalles Dam, possibly Tsagiglalal in her long-eared guise. Or the wavy beard could indicate a water monster. On page 61, Spedis Owl is incised into the wall of Petroglyph Canyon near Skamania, Oregon. The Wishram say that Spedis Owl married a cannibal woman who steals children. There are many versions of his image.

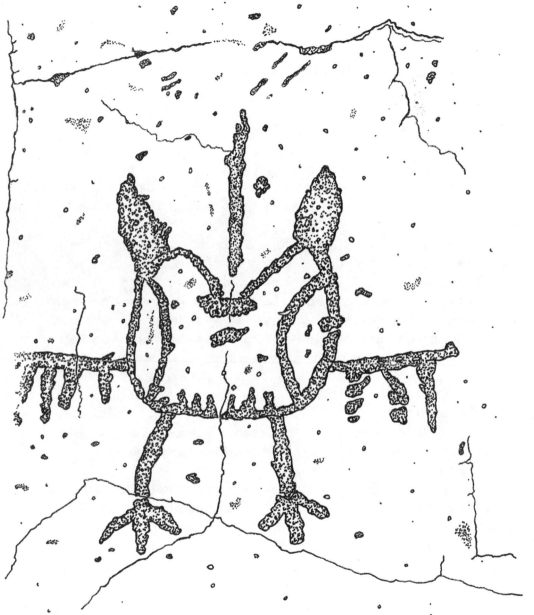

Pictograph has come to mean an image painted on rock, rather than pecked or grooved. In the Southwest, pictographs are mostly red or yellow, but artists used a broader range of colors in the Columbia Plateau: red, white, green, yellow, black. Sometimes the paint was applied or printed with fingers, like the handprints in the Southwest or the dots on Arctic masks. Sometimes the color was blown through a tube. Archaeologists excavating Bernard Creek Rock Shelter in Hell's Canyon, Idaho, have found bird bone "tubes" with traces of red pigment inside. Artists at the Pecos River caves in Texas wrapped sotol leaves in bundles and shredded the ends to make brushes similar to the yucca fiber brushes used by potters.

Paints have always been made from earth pigments. They are among the most permanent of colors, the only difference today is the binder. The pigment was applied dry or sometimes with a vehicle—water or liquid from cactus or other plants. Pecos River artists made crayons by adding grease or fat to the ground earth. How have these pure pigments survived? Studies show that the pigment binds chemically to the rock.

Dating is difficult in rock art—you can't carbon date stone. But scholars deduce from related evidence that can be dated, such as preserved wooden roof beams. At Bernard Creek, Idaho, for instance, scientists found flaked stones from ancient walls with traces of red and were able to date that layer of the dig at about 6,000 years ago. Images can also give a clue, the date of the introduction of the horse, or an atlatl or a bow and arrow or the sudden proliferation of kachina images, or a person with a hat. There are also stylistic differences; rock art has "art movements" as distinct as Impressionism from Dada, usually dated by comparison with pottery styles.

There are more pictographs than petroglyphs in parts of the Columbia Plateau. This painted figure near Bend, Oregon, has a gesture similar to the "barbell" men in Idaho, but the arms are extended, not raised. Is the person pregnant or merely round? The large rectangles suggest eyes, but they could simply be geometric forms.

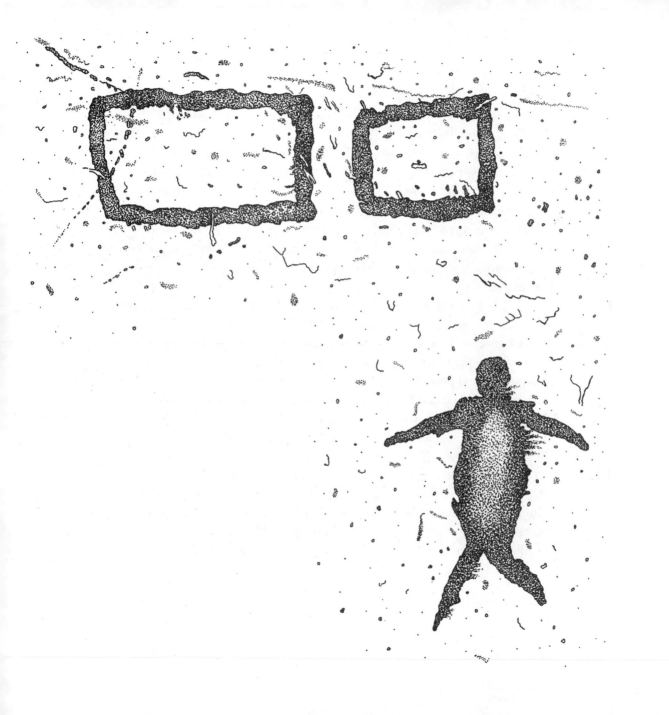

This image probably appeared in the vision of a Salish or Kutenai teenager who had come to this remote place near Keremos Creek, British Columbia, to seek a personal guardian spirit. The pilgrim would sit within a circle of stones to pray and fast, awaiting a vision. The guardian spirit could appear in any form—animal, rock, plant, person—and bestow a special song to help in difficult moments. Often a seeker would choose a place where others had prayed, leaving painted records of their own visions. The new dreamer would add a fresh image. Places with paintings were considered sacred. This boulder has only one person's vision, a mask-like face.

The twins on page 66 may have been pecked during a vision quest. The rayed arcs above their heads attest to their spiritual power. The small central figure could be the seeker. There are many petroglyph versions of spirit twins in the Columbia Plateau. Some Salish people felt human twins possessed special powers as well and called them "grizzly bear children." Further east, the Lakota Sioux depicted a similar spirit called Double Woman, also twinned, with a child in the middle. Double Woman's spiritual headdress is a pair of horns; she is the patron of quill-workers. This petroglyph has lost its remote location; it can be seen at Ginkgo Petrified Forest State Park Museum in Vantage, Washington.

The spirit figure on page 67 is surrounded by halos and dots of visionary power. A later seeker probably added the modest stick figure touching the toe of the supernatural. To no avail. This petroglyph on the Columbia River near Beverly, Washington, has been destroyed, joining at least forty-five nearby rock art sites lost to dams or road construction.

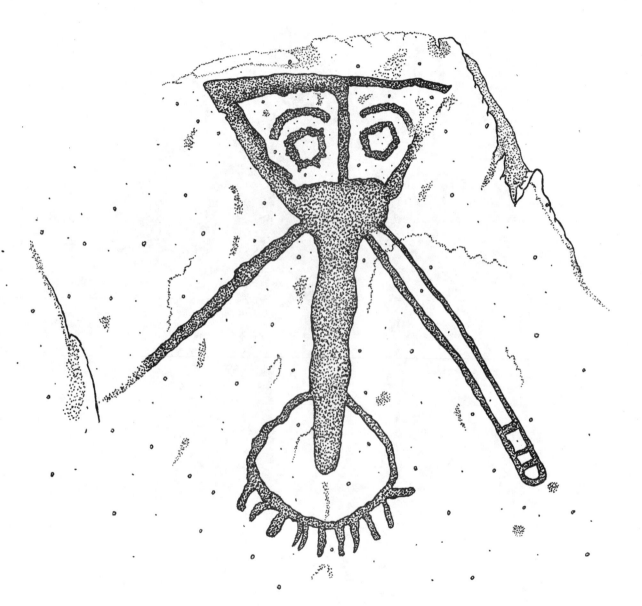

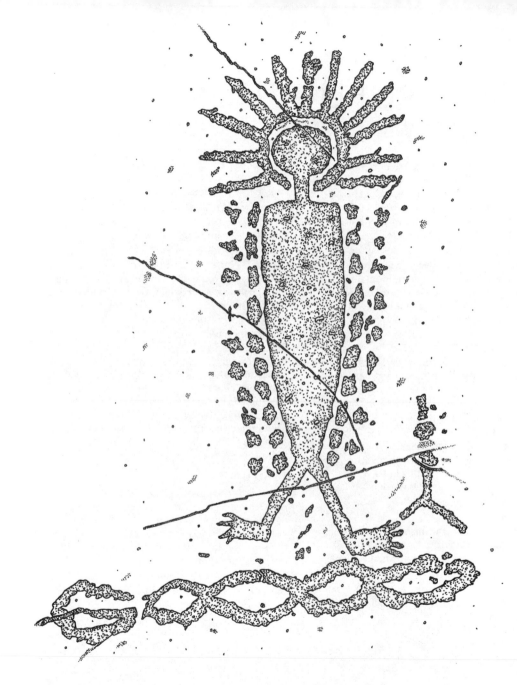

PUBLIC SITES

Asterisk denotes a site discussed or illustrated in the previous section.

CALIFORNIA

Anza Borrego Desert State Park Pictograph Site
A 600,000-acre public park open all year, 90 miles east of San Diego at Borrego Springs. Fluid black, yellow, and red pictographs and petroglyphs related to the Cahuilla and Kumeyay people are visible from a self-guided one-mile trail.

Blythe Intaglios
Giant incised figures, some over 175 feet long, always visible across the desert floor. From Blythe, drive 17 miles north on U.S. 95 to the marker for "Giant Desert Figures." Approach this site with care; vandals have driven over the huge figures with trucks.

Chumash Painted Cave*
Polychrome paintings with sun symbols visible through a protective grill. From Santa Barbara, continue on California 154 to junction with Painted Cave Road, then drive 4 miles further to marker.

Death Valley National Monument
Petroglyphs at Klare Spring, Titus Canyon, Greenwater Canyon, Mesquite Springs Campground, and Emigrant Canyon made by people occupying the area starting in 6000 B.C. Located off Route 190, 110 miles north of Ridgecrest, the park is always open.

Hemet Maze Stone
A single fenced boulder embellished with a maze, located in a small Riverside County park on California Avenue about 3 miles north of Hemet.

Indian Grinding Stone State Historic Park*
Petroglyphs near a reconstructed Miwok village, located on Volcano Road off Highway 88 at Pine Grove.

Inscription Canyon (also called Black Canyon)
Numerous petroglyphs on basalt cliffs, northwest of Barstow. Contact Bureau of Land Management in Barstow for directions.

Joshua Tree National Monument
Pictographs and petroglyphs by Serrano, Chemehuevi, and Cahuilla peoples. Visitors' center is in Twentynine Palms.

Lava Beds National Monument
This site is sacred to contemporary Modoc people. Petroglyphs are near Skull Cave, Big Painted Cave, and Symbol Bridge. Drive 9 miles south on California 139 from Tulelake.

Little Petroglyph Canyon
(also called Renegade Canyon)*
Over 20,0000 rock drawings made by Coso Range ancestors of the Shoshone, dating from 11,000 years ago. This magnificent site is located within the China Lake Naval Weapons Center so you can only visit on a weekend tour conducted by the Maturango Museum. Write to Maturango Museum of Indian Wells Valley, P.O. Box 1776, Ridgecrest, California 93556.

NEVADA

Grimes Point Archaeological Area
Archaeological sites dating from 8,000 years ago around an ancient lake bed, with rock art through-out the area. Grimes Point Petroglyph Trail is well marked. The area is located at Grimes Point, 12 miles east of Fallon on Highway 50. It is open daily.

Hickison Summit Petroglyphs
Self-guided trail with petroglyphs. Drive 24 miles east on U.S. 50 from Austin.

Lake Mead Recreation Area

Many fine petroglyphs made during 11,000 years of habitation visible at Grapevine Wash, on Christmas Tree Pass Road, near Davis Dam, and on Lake Mohave. Others are now underwater. Lake Mead can be reached by highway from Las Vegas or Glendale.

IDAHO

Alpha Rockshelter

Pictographs on the roof of a rock shelter located near North Fork, about 20 miles north of Salmon on U.S. 93. Follow the Forest Service Road along the Salmon River past Shoup, cross Pine Creek Bridge, and continue along the river 4 miles to the site marker.

Birds of Prey Natural Area*

A canyon with many petroglyphs along the Snake River and inside Celebration Park to the north. Always open, the area is located south of Melba along the Snake River. Contact the Bureau of Land Management in Boise for more information.

McCammon Petroglyphs

Rock art on boulders near a fence and along the Snake River. The sites are located 18 miles southeast of Pocatello on Interstate 15 near the rest stop for McCammon.

Wes Bar Petroglyphs

Spectacular site at Swan Falls Dam on Snake River near Kuna, visible by boat or on foot about 3.5 miles downriver. Wes Bar is listed on the National Register of Historic Places.

OREGON

Hell's Canyon National Recreation Area*

Huge park with over 200 rock art sites, located along the Snake River in both Oregon and Idaho. The Forest Service in Enterprise distributes a brochure on the park. To visit the petroglyphs at Buffalo Eddy,* drive south on Washington 129 from Clarkson, Washington, through Asotin to Snake River Road. The petroglyphs are visible after driving along the road about 18 miles.

UTAH (For other sites in Utah, see *Southwest*)

Newspaper Rock State Park*

Layers of drawings on a cliff face made by Ute, Anasazi, and Fremont artists over a 1,500-year period. From Monticello, drive 14 miles north on Highway 191, then take Route 211, 14 miles to the park, which is always open.

Potash Road Petroglyphs

Two miles of rock art panels by both Ute and Fremont artists. The petroglyphs are located 8 miles west of Moab on Utah 279.

WASHINGTON

Horsethief Lake State Park*

Rock art along the Columbia River, including the drawing of Tsagiglalal. Cross the Columbia River at the Dalles; at the junction of Highways 197 and 14, turn east on Highway 14; from there it is 2 miles to the park entrance.

Ginkgo Petrified Forest State Park*

Fragments of petroglyphs salvaged from three dam sites along the Columbia River. The museum is located off Interstate 90 at Vantage.

Indian Painted Rocks
(also called *Little Spokane Pictographs*)

There are two pictograph sites. One is located on the Spokane River about 6 miles past the town of Tumtum on Highway 291. The other is along Little Spokane River near Rutter Parkway Bridge. Washington State Parks and Recreation administers both sites.

Roosevelt Petroglyphs

Another park with salvaged petroglyphs from the John Jay Dam. It is located on Washington Highway 14, one mile east of Roosevelt.

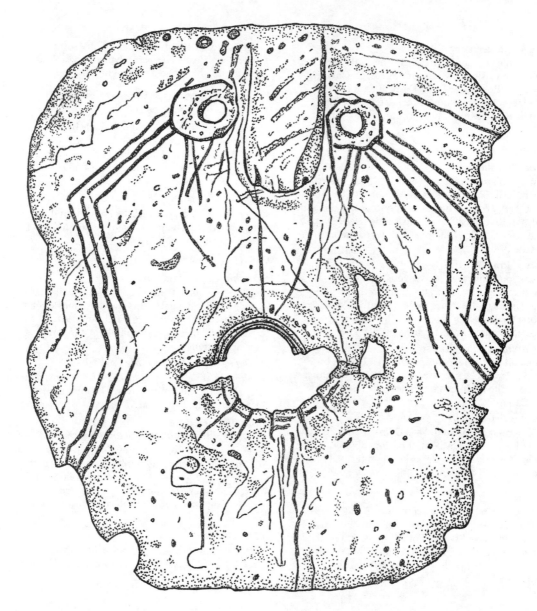

MISSISSIPPI RIVER
AND THE SOUTHEAST

The Mississippi River was a roadway for the ancient Caddoan people whose home was near the Arkansas and Red Rivers in Oklahoma. They built great earthen mounds along the Arkansas River at Spiro to serve as platforms for elaborate mortuaries, temples, or political centers. The earthworks of the Mound Builders "grew" over the centuries in cycles of ritual renewal. Caddoans would periodically raze the structures, cover the mound with a fresh layer of dirt, then rebuild. People lived in the valleys nearby, raising corn and squash and hunting small game. Trade extended up the Mississippi and its tributaries past Cahokia in Missouri; south as far as Florida and Louisiana; east into Alabama, Georgia, and Tennessee. The Caddoans sent rabbit-hair yarn and buffalo wool south; they received copper from the Great Lakes, whelk shells from the Florida Keys, and the Gulf Coast. Scholars trace some shells found at Spiro to the coasts of Veracruz and Yucatan. The Caddoans incised these shells with drawings—I think of their works as watery "petroglyphs." Artists smoothed the shell, then carved lines with a stone tool, like drawing on rock. The lines were darkened with pigment. They made shell cups, round shell gorgets worn as pendants, and shell masks.

This small mask from the Craig Mound at Spiro could be held in your hand or worn as a necklace. The mouth of the mask was hollowed open from the natural tip of the whelk. It has thunderbolt lines extending from the eyes, a symbol associated with the falcon-like prowess of warriors. The zigzags are also related to the power of fire—Thunderbird gave people fire by sending down a lightning bolt. The mask probably dates from the thirteenth or fourteenth centuries.

In 1838, the Choctaws, like their Cherokee neighbors in the Southeast, were forced to resettle in eastern Oklahoma, a cruel reversal of the old trade routes. They ended up near Spiro, where the abandoned temple mounds of the Caddoans remained visible only as earthen hills. A century later, these mounds were crudely excavated by the Pocola Mining Company, and the shell engravings scattered into private collections. The Oklahoma legislature stopped the looting after two years, passing an antiquities act in 1934, but the damage was done. Anthropologist Forrest E. Clements describes the scene: "The great mound had been tunneled through and through, gutted in a frenzy of haste. . . . Sections of cedar poles lay scattered on the ground, fragments of feather and fur textiles littered the whole area; it was impossible to take a single step . . . without scuffing up broken pieces of pottery, sections of engraved shell, and beads of shell, stone and bone" (Phillips 1978, p. 5).

These hands face the viewer in a permanent gesture of self-examination. The circle with the cross in each palm could symbolize the sun; it could represent political power as well. The Natchez, neighboring Mound Builders to the south, called their leader "Great Sun" and kept a sacred fire, fed by four logs, burning in the central temple. The images on these hands from Spiro could represent a similar religious concept.

Some scholars were startled by the "severed" hands and heads found at these mortuary sites and concluded that the Caddoans had been enthusiastic sacrificers. Not so. When an important person died, Mississippians would have a second ceremony in later years, removing the hands and head for a ritual re-burial that transformed an individual into a sacred ancestor.

The hand with an eye on page 74 is engraved on a shell from Spiro. The petroglyph on page 75 was pecked near the Purgatoire River in southeastern Colorado before the twelfth century. Caddoan imagery was often incorporated into Plains Indian iconography. Both drawings are right hands backed by a "seeing" eye.

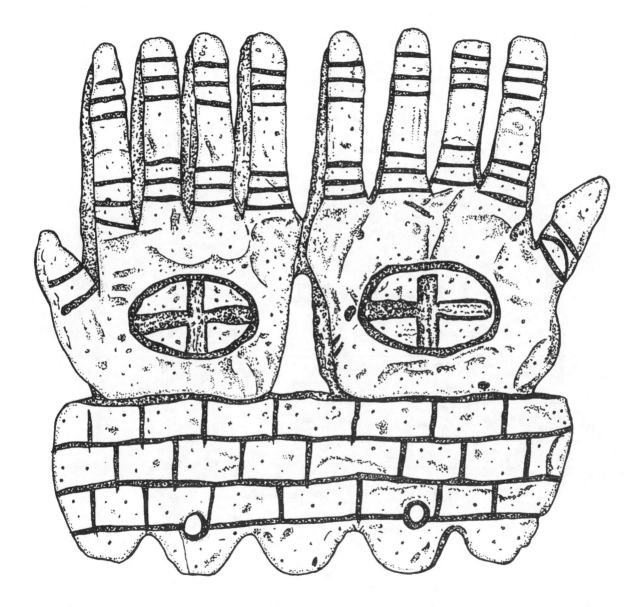

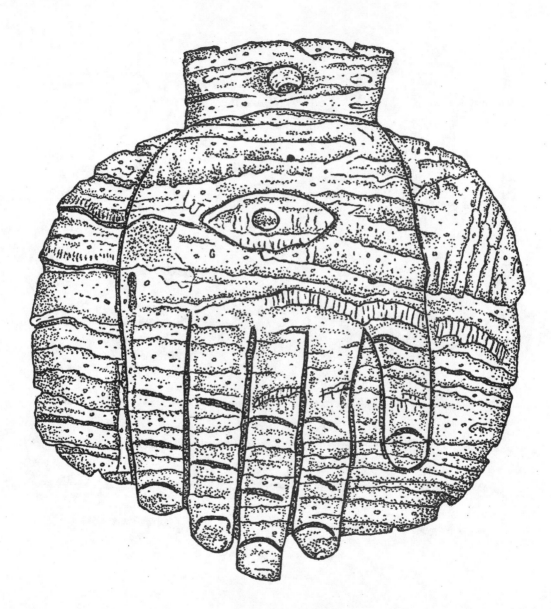

The swirling birds on this shell gorget from Spiro could be woodpeckers or herons. Rotating around a sun symbol swastika, they could also represent the four directions. Other cultures have interpreted this symbol as migration. Writer Frank Waters describes the migration concepts in Hopi swastikas, "Upon arriving at each *paso* all the leading clans turned right before retracing their routes. . . . This transformed the cross into a great swastika rotating counterclockwise to indicate the earth . . ." (Waters 1963, pp. 113–14). This disc was carved in the thirteenth or fourteenth centuries.

Nineteenth-century settlers along the Mississippi had their own fanciful migration stories to "explain" the earthen mounds left by Caddoans, Mississippians, and other woodland peoples. They named their towns Cairo or Memphis because they imagined that Egyptians had created the earthworks, not the indigenous people they had displaced. St. Louis was built near Cahokia, a Mississippian town whose largest ceremonial mound was as big as the Pyramid of Cheops at its base. Photographer Thomas Easterly recorded the removal of the last mound in St. Louis with a photo series of diminishing views of "Big Mound," located at Fifth and Mound Streets, 1868–1869. The town people came to watch as the mound was razed. Easterly describes the "eager boys . . . who scrambled for the beads which were thrown out with every handful of dirt . . ." (Kilgo 1994, p. 206). Despite the discovery of skeletons, shell artifacts, and copper masks, many refused to believe that the Big Mound had been constructed. Elihu Shepard, a founder of the Missouri Historical Society, insisted that the Big Mound was a "work of nature only" containing "many small, rude and trifling ornaments" (Kilgo 1994, p. 206).

Ornately incised shells from Spiro were used as ritual cups, engraved with images of Caddoan cosmology. Here is the rattlesnake again, this time in the guise of two intertwined snake dancers. Some scholars associate paired snakes with a Creek myth that tells of Corn Mother weaving a crown of snakes and bluejay feathers for her hero son. Here the twisted snakes are long cloaks in the shape of tails. The dancer on the right is carrying a snake staff in one hand, a knife in the other. The thumbs are reversed on both hands. Is the man a warrior? The raccoon below the dancer's feet may be an animal spirit for a military society. We can see the foot of the second dancer, who faces in the opposite direction. One snake skin is an obvious rattlesnake pattern, but the other one is spotted like a panther.

The drawing on page 80 shows a figure called a *piasa*. This is a composite panther-snake-bird-human, a sacred combination that unites the upper, middle, and lower worlds. The figures wear similar ornaments—earrings, shell bracelets. The *piasa* has a panther eye that resembles the falcon symbol drawn around the eyes of warriors.

A description of the *piasa* first comes to us from Father Jacques Marquette in the seventeenth century. Indian parishioners had warned him about "monsters" in the river. From the banks of the Mississippi near the Illinois and Missouri Rivers he spied a pictograph of "two painted monsters which at first made us afraid. . . . They are as large as a calf; they have horns on their heads like those of a deer, a horrible look, red eyes, a beard like a tiger's, a face somewhat like a man's, a body covered with scales, and so long a tail that it winds all around the body passing above the head and going back between the legs, ending in a fish's tail" (Brose 1985, p. 127). He had seen images of the underwater panther sacred to Great Lakes people, like the one incised on this cup of the Caddoans.

Not all cups depict supernaturals. The cup facing the *piasa* (page 81) is engraved with a tree. This is one of only two images of trees found at Spiro. All three cups date from the thirteenth to fourteenth centuries.

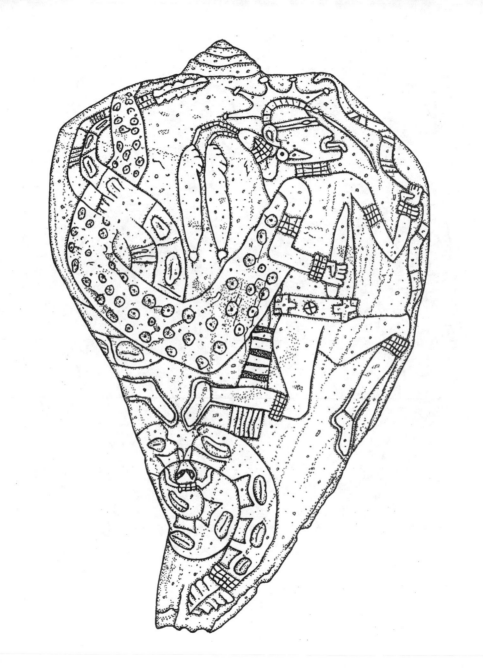

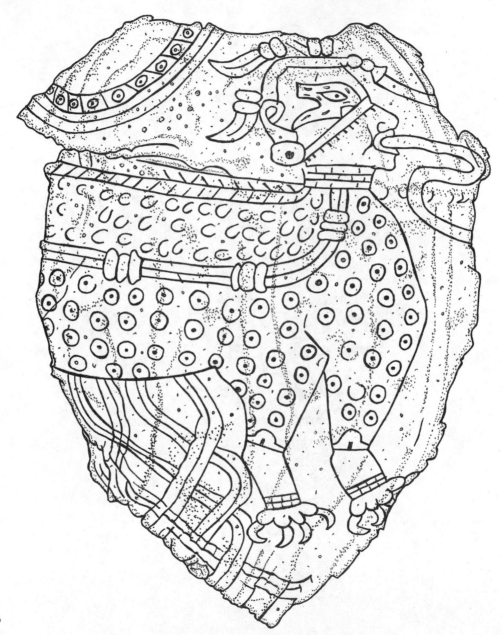

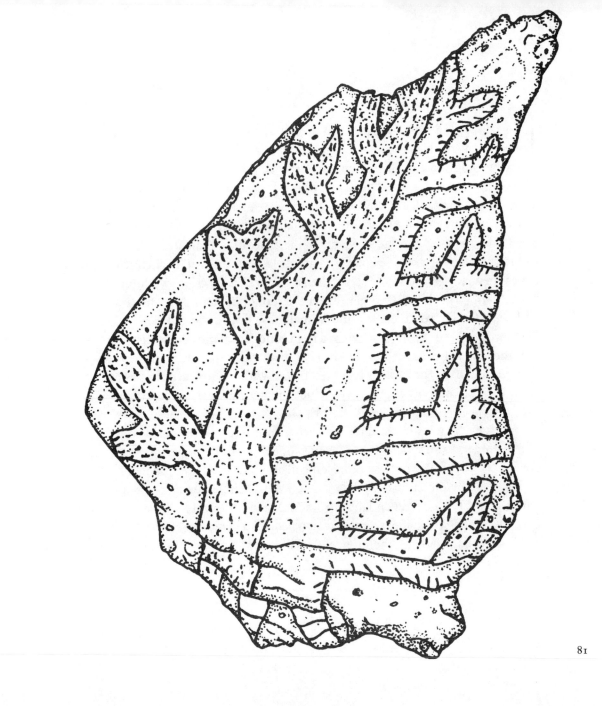

Hernando de Soto passed through the Southeast in the sixteenth century. He led a small army of men, horses, and dogs along the old river routes from the Gulf Coast in Florida up into Georgia, the Carolinas, Tennessee, Mississippi, Alabama, and Louisiana, where de Soto died of a fever. His party were hoping for gold, but they found river pearls, seashells, and numerous Natives who fought the army or discreetly directed them further inland, away from their towns. The survivors of the expedition managed to get to Mexico, then home to Spain. Garcilaso de la Vega, known as The Inca, heard their stories and wrote about their journey. He describes a temple at Cofachiqui, probably in Georgia: "Over the roof of the temple many large and small shells of different marine animals have been arranged. The Spaniards did not learn how they had been brought inland, but it may be that they too are produced in the rivers of that land which are so numerous and full of water. These shells had been placed with the inside out so as to show their greatest luster and they included many conch shells of strange magnificence" (de la Vega 1980, p. 314).

This highly stylized rattlesnake coils counterclockwise inside a shell gorget. Its mouth is the "v"-shaped opening on the right, the eye a concentric circle. The rattles on the left coil downward. The four small circles could be directional. Spirals and concentric circles are associated with water. This incised pendant is from McMahon Mound in Sevier County, Tennessee, made by Appalachian peoples a century before de Soto's encounter with their descendants.

83

This fish-like marine shell mask made in the sixteenth or seventeenth centuries was found at the Little Egypt site in Murray County, Georgia. Archaeologists call the facial marks a "weeping eye" motif, but the lines have nothing to do with sorrow. The marks are lightning bolts with falcon-like lines around the eyes. This is the face of a powerful ancestor spirit.

The Mound Builder cultures declined after the seventeenth century but their influence was felt both among their southeastern descendants and the Plains people to the west. Mississippian shell masks were used in the war bundles of Kansa people to evoke an ancestor's sacred assistance. In a 1915 study, ethnologist Alanson Skinner describes the mourning rituals for a deceased Kansa warrior. After an appropriate period of mourning, a war party would set out. "Before going into battle, the sacred bundle was opened and the two braves took from it the hawk or the seashell (mask) and the reed and basket wrappers. The two warriors who did this thereby pledged themselves to kill an enemy or die in the attempt. These badges were hung around their necks by the leaders, who removed the charms at night before the party slept" (Skinner 1915, p. 749).

Where did the Mound Builders go? The descendants of the Caddoans include the Wichita and the Caddo in East Texas. Chickasaw, Choctaw, Creek, Cherokee, Seminole, Catawba, Yuchi, Quapaw, Natchez, and Tuscarora are all related to ancestral Mississippians.

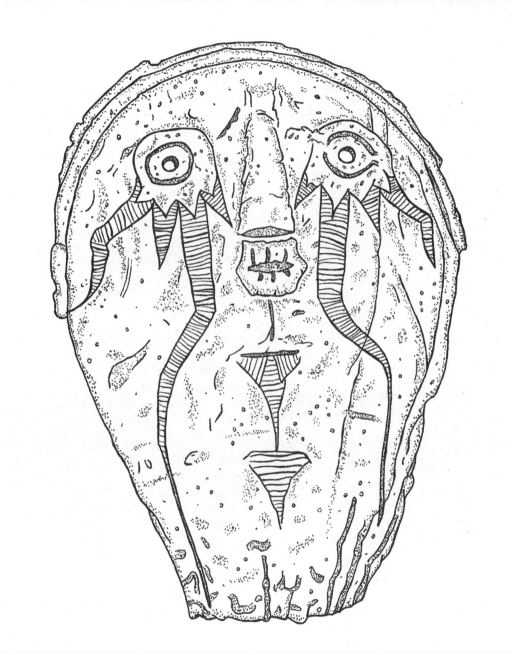

PUBLIC SITES

Asterisk denotes a site discussed or illustrated in the previous sections.

ALABAMA

Moundville Archaeological Park

A restored mound site off Route 69 just north of Moundville with a museum featuring incised shell artifacts.

ARKANSAS

Hampton Museum State Park

Located 44 miles north of Wilson on U.S. 61, this museum displays incised Mississippian shell ornaments and other artifacts from the Nodena site.

Henderson State University Museum

A museum and archaeological area featuring Caddoan incised pottery and artifacts, located in Arkadelphia.

FLORIDA

Crystal River State Archaeological Site

The site includes three mounds and an engraved stone stele. It is located along Route 3 in Crystal River.

GEORGIA

Etowah Mounds State Historic Site

A restored mound site with a museum of artifacts and petroglyphs. It is located along Route 2 in Cartersville.

Rock Eagle Effigy Mound

An earthwork 120 feet long, shaped like an eagle or buzzard. It is located on Rock Eagle Road in Eatonton.

Track Rock Archaeological Area

This site is a 52-acre preserve within the Chattahoochee National Forest located on Track Rock Road 1½ miles south of U.S. 76 near Blairsville. There are rock carvings.

ILLINOIS*

Cahokia Mounds State Historic Site

Located near Collinsville, this major site has several excavated earthworks.

LOUISIANA

Poverty Point State Commemorative Area

This huge mound site 15 miles north of Delhi on Route 577 dates from 1500 B.C. and is shaped like a bird.

MISSISSIPPI

Winterville Mound State Park

A ceremonial mound from the thirteenth century and a museum with incised artifacts. Follow Route 1, 10 miles north of Greenville. See also Missouri listing after *Great Plains* section.

NORTH CAROLINA

Town Creek Indian Mound State Historic Site

A restored painting is inside a restored temple. The site is located on Route 3 in Mt. Gilead.

Juttaculla Rock

A boulder with many patterned petroglyphs. It is located on private land near a branch of the Tuckasegee River above Webster. Obtain permission from owner to visit.

OKLAHOMA

Rock Art Research Center

Visit the Thunderbird Library at Rogers State College in Claremont for photos and directions to Oklahoma rock art sites.

Spiro Mounds Archaeological Site*

Partially restored mortuary mounds. Travel 6 miles northeast of Spiro on Spiro Mounds Road. You can view the incised shells at the University of Oklahoma Museum of Natural History in Norman.

TENNESSEE

Pinson Mound State Archaeological Site

This impressive mound with many incised shell artifacts is on Ozier Road in Pinson.

WEST VIRGINIA

Grave Creek Mound State Park
(also called Mammoth Mound)

Adena mound site plus a small museum with artifacts and the famous hoax petroglyph, the Grave Creek Stone. It is located at 801 Jefferson Street, one block east of Route 2 in Moundsville.

Sculptured Rocks

There may still be rock art along the Guyandotte River, drawn and photographed in nineteenth-century publications.

GREAT PLAINS

The Great Plains is a gigantic grassland that extends from Alberta and Saskatchewan in Canada south into Texas. Picture whole villages moving from their summer garden sites to follow the buffalo herds, dogs dragging the lodge poles, women setting up tipis at traditional locations. Or great towns of woven-grass houses, or conical earth lodges grouped on high cliffs above the Missouri River to the north.

Rock art followed these routes, usually near places with water or in secluded locations for spiritual retreat. It was ceremonial art peopled with animals, supernaturals, and abstract imagery, or narrative art with warriors and battle scenes. The Great Plains was a place of shifting populations; new settlers honored the power of these ancient drawing sites, often adding their own images. A Cheyenne told ethnologist George Bird Grinnell that the rock drawings were places of power because they appeared "without anyone having painted them." The Gros Ventre attributed some of the petroglyphs to people, but others to supernatural "ghost men" or "little people." Who were the artists? Blackfeet, Gros Ventre, Hidatsa, Mandan, Arikara, Cheyenne, Ponca, Omaha, Iowa, Pawnee, Arapaho, Kansa, Kiowa, Missouri, Osage, Wichita, Comanche, Tonkawa, Crow, Shoshone, Minniconjou, Quapaw, Kitsai, Assiniboin, Nez Perce, Oto, Piegan, the various branches of the Sioux—Lakota, Dakota, Nakota.

This horse and rider were pecked over a frieze of older images near the Purgatoire River in southeastern Colorado. The petroglyph probably dates from the seventeenth century, shortly after Plains people began capturing horses from Spanish settlements in neighboring Mexico. They called the new animals "sky dogs." The man is standing with a horse superimposed, an early convention for a rider. In later pictographs, the rider is drawn astraddle. The eroded older images behind the horse are agricultural—corn, marks which could be calendar counts, erotic couples. The rider is poised against his new mobility.

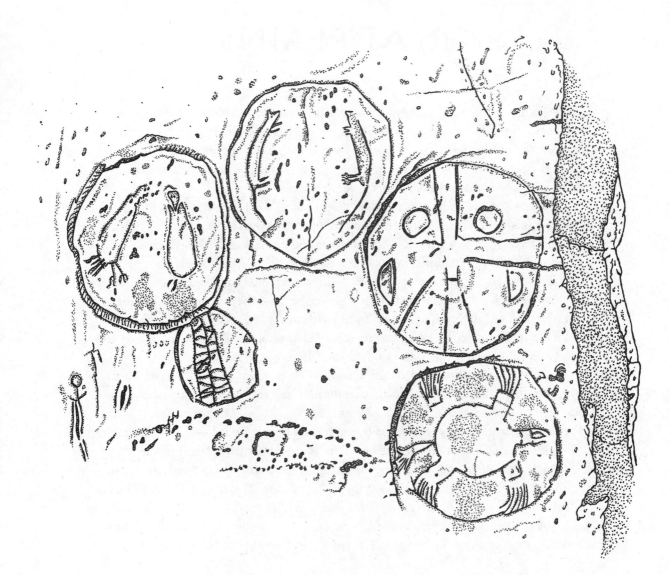

A successful warrior needed more than fighting skill; he needed the protective songs and images of a personal spirit guardian. The images on these pecked shields were received through fast-induced visions. The power belonged only to the seeker; the image could not be copied by another. There are twelve shields incised into a sandstone wall at verdant Castle Gardens, Wyoming, each with its individual vision painting. The shields are actual size, two or three feet in diameter, like the rawhide originals. The artists were probably Shoshone men, but Plains warriors also included "manly-hearted women" who had a special calling for warfare.

Guardian spirits are frequently animals. The pair on the middle shield could be otters; the birds on the fringed shield look like prairie hens or vultures. I see a turtle in the lower shield, but some scholars see six bear paws radiating in a circle. Either is a powerful spirit—bear paws are identified with healing; the turtle is a world symbol.

The shields are round, like the cosmos. Plains people made their houses round, arranged in concentric circles in the village; even the objects inside the lodges were placed to mimic the world directions. The symbolism went both ways. The Sioux believed that the sun, moon, and earth were round like a shield.

Shield-bearing warriors from Writing-On-Stone Provincial Park, Alberta are shown on pages 92 and 93. The name derives from the Blackfeet phrase *aysin'eep,* "it has been written." The images are incised on rock formations sculpted by Milk River as it flows down into Montana. Like the shields in Wyoming, these warrior images predate the horse. The Shoshone preceded the equestrian Blackfeet and Gros Ventre in this region and probably pecked these drawings between the fourteenth and eighteenth centuries. Notice the elaborate headdresses and size of the shields; the people are dwarfed in importance by their regalia.

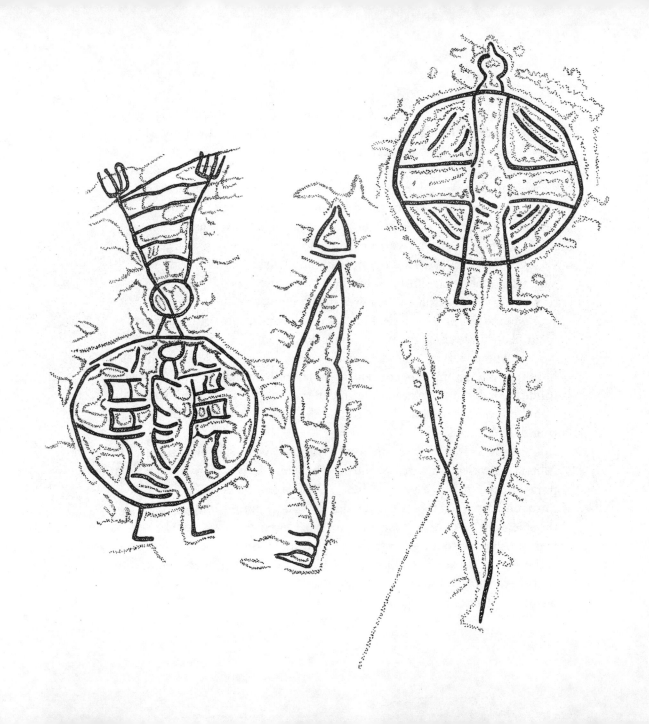

Birds inhabit both land and air; all birds could be seen as potential messengers between humans and the sky deities. Thunderbird is an important supernatural for both Plains and Great Lakes peoples. He is frequently depicted emitting lightning bolts or radiating wavy lines of spiritual energy and is identified with the life-giving power of storms. Writer Richard Erdoes recorded Brule Sioux medicine man James (Fire) Lame Deer in 1969, talking about Thunderbird: "He loves what is clean and pure. His voice is the great thunderclap and the smaller rolling thunders that follow his booming shouts are the cries of his children" (Erdoes 1984, p. 219).

This Thunderbird is incised on rocks in southeastern Colorado, traditional home of the Southern Cheyenne and the Arapaho. It has a heart line from the mouth to the heart, a symbol of spiritual vitality borrowed from the Great Lakes, where some Plains people originated.

The Thunderbird has migrated into contemporary American culture as well. The Farm Workers Union has adopted this powerful image in their struggle for decent wages and working conditions. A commercialized version is found in the fancy "T" bird car of the 1950s, symbol of a different kind of power.

This petroglyph is incised into a rock at Castle Butte, Montana. It's a large tipi, nine poles in profile, possibly eighteen in the round. The drawing was probably pecked after horse transport allowed people to enlarge the size of their lodges. The traditional dog travois limited the number and length of poles. Francisco de Coronado, venturing into the Plains from Mexico in 1541, noticed the marks made by the dragging poles before he encountered the camp of Apache hunters with its circle of "tall and beautiful" tipis. Ring lines left by tipis are often found near petroglyph sites. This mobile architecture left its permanent traces.

Women erected the lodges, prepared and sewed the buffalo skin coverings, and sometimes painted the abstract patterns that bordered a tipi at the top and bottom. A woman might also quill stars and rosettes on the lodges by sewing dyed porcupine quills into patterns. Women had quill-worker societies analogous to men's military societies. Ethnologist George Bird Grinnell described a Northern Cheyenne meeting. "At all meetings of these quillers, before the food was served, it was usual for one old woman after another to get up and tell of the robes she had quilled, just as a warrior would recount his brave deeds" (Grinnell 1923, p. 165–66). A woman may have pecked this image as well. She could have been Blackfeet, Crow, or Gros Ventre.

Some tipis were ornamented with personal vision paintings or military narratives in the central area between the borders. The visions were painted by men and "owned" by the dreamer. They were powerful images that protected the occupants of the lodge. A particular vision could be inherited or assigned to another, a Plains version of spiritual copyright. If a painted tipi became worn, a woman would make a new covering. The owner of the vision would invite other men to "renew" the tipi by repainting the same images— a form of conceptual art in which the image mattered more than the person who rendered the drawing.

Pueblo villages in northern New Mexico, including Taos and San Juan, now have small buffalo herds, part of the cultural renaissance of Pueblo spiritual life.

Buffalo were the principal animal of the Plains and their importance extended west and south to other Native cultures. Buffalo were literally the source of life, providing food, tipi coverings, robes, shirts—even the bones were used as hoes. Lakota women frequently painted their summer buffalo robes with a geometric border-and-box pattern that symbolized the food-giving insides of the animal. Many tribes had buffalo societies for men and women.

This white pictograph is painted against the dark stone of Indian Head Canyon, overlooking the Lemhi Mountains and Birch Creek Valley in eastern Idaho. Archaeologist Max G. Pavesic suggests that a Shoshone shaman created this image during a quest for spiritual renewal. The horns and gesture depict his power. Like the Gros Ventre, Shoshone believed in a tribe of "little people" called Nunumbis, hunters dressed in goat skin, carrying tiny quivers of arrows. They drew on rocks, hid in caves, and could bestow shamanistic powers, but there is nothing miniature in this painting.

The petroglyph on page 100 is from Ludlow Cave in the South Cave Hills of South Dakota. Sioux artists probably pecked this ambiguous cow; is she a two-humped buffalo or a range cow? She contains a tiny buffalo and nurses a buffalo calf. Could this be a transitional image as range cattle replaced the decimated buffalo herds?

The Colorado petroglyph shown on page 101 contains warrior symbolism—a buffalo with an eroded star in his belly, similar to the imagery of the Mandan and Hidatsa Bull's Society that associated the buffalo with Morning Star. An analogous women's society honored the female deity White Buffalo Cow.

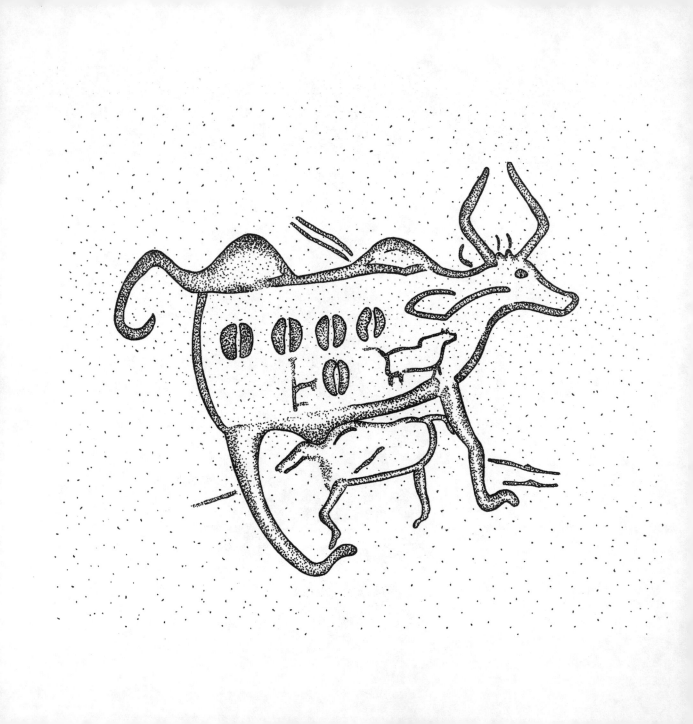

You often see a solitary hand depicted in Plains art—usually a symbol for "counting coup" or striking. Plains warriors had an elaborate system of war honors. Touching an enemy simply by hand was the ultimate bravery, though there were other means of counting coup. Some warriors carried a coup stick into battle, often adorned with a carving of an enemy soldier, and tried to reach out during battle to strike an adversary. Of course, a warrior could "touch" harder, with a spear, a club, an arrow, and kill the person. This too was counting coup. The respect for courage extended to the enemy fighter. If a very brave man was killed, many would come to count coup over his body and symbolically imbibe his bravery.

This southeastern Colorado rock embellished with hands and feet could be related to coup symbolism. Incised hands appear in rock art throughout the continent; the meaning varies with the culture. If these hands had been pecked by a Navajo, they might be prayers. Ethnologist Gladys A. Reichard observed people praying at petroglyphs by placing their hands into the incised prints. A coup symbol is connected with prayer as well—a person's success in battle was an indication of the strength of his spirit helper.

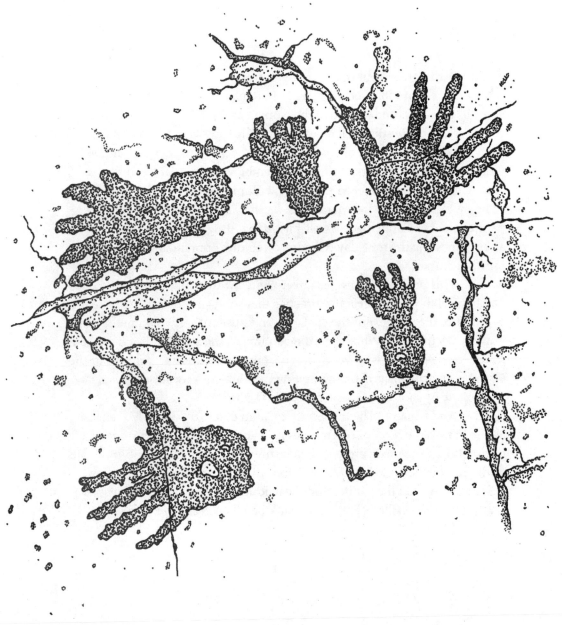

Scholars disagree about this petroglyph from Picture Canyon, Baca County, Colorado. Archaeologist E. B. Renaud looked at the pattern of spots in the 1930s and identified the woman as a smallpox sufferer. But recent scholars question that assumption. The spots could be a costume. They are linked like rows of chain. She has no lesions on her face and is wearing a headdress. Some think she resembles ceremonial figures from New Mexico or the Upper Missouri—the Zuni Fire God Shulawitsi or "The Evil Spirit" from the Mandan *O-kee-pa* ritual. Nineteenth-century painter George Catlin made a well-known painting of the spotted figure after witnessing the four-day religious ceremony dramatizing Mandan creation stories.

This petroglyph has been overprinted with chalk, making the lines harsh. Chalking is a destructive practice that some photographers have used to enhance the image. But the chalk doesn't dust out—it's a pigment and bonds with the rock. While recording an image, the art lover has distorted it. A petroglyph is a visual ventriloquist. Like the Lilliputian painters of the Gros Ventre, the magical pictographs appear and disappear but the chalked ones made by mortals are visible in plain daylight.

And what of "The Evil Spirit"? Catlin describes the 1832 scene in a letter. "The old master of ceremonies . . . had met this monster of fiends, and having thrust the medicine-pipe before him, held him still and immovable under its charm!" (Catlin 1973, Vol. I, p. 167). The prosperous Mandan village that hosted the painter and theatrically repelled evil was struck five years later by a smallpox epidemic that killed 90 percent of the villagers.

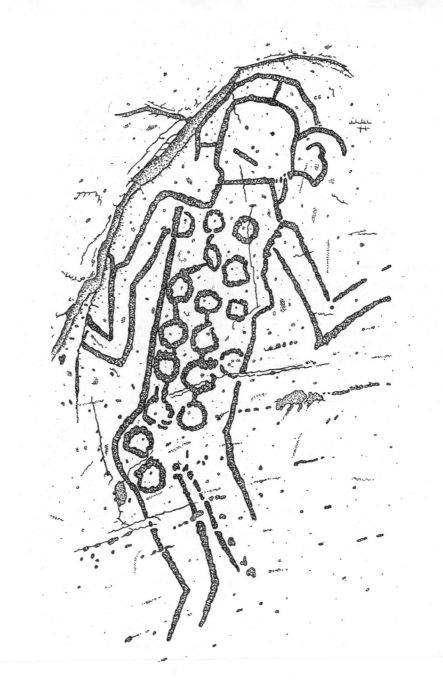

People lived along the Pecos River in Texas for 9,000 years, occupying rock shelters and creating lasting art inside caves and along the canyon walls. Artists from each cultural layering left their marks, Apache, Comanche, Cibola, Jumano, Kiowa, Kickapoo. The hunter-gatherer inhabitants who created the earlier art didn't leave their names. The caves are adorned with polychrome paintings of mountain lion deities posed in profile above tall human figures facing the viewer, waving their arms. The abstract lines surrounding the figures would make a twentieth-century Expressionist painter feel at home. This mountain lion is painted in red on the walls of Seminole Canyon Shelter, probably after 3000 B.C. The artist used brushes made from the sotol plant. Many of the feline deities are depicted standing with the front legs outstretched, like this prickly tailed cat.

Animals from a later period are shown on the next pages. A richly antlered mountain sheep (page 108) and a bull elk (page 109) were pecked along the walls of Legend Rock, Wyoming, by Shoshone artists between the seventeenth and eighteenth centuries. Both are endowed with erotic and spiritual power. The bull elk was a gallant and irresistible fellow for the Lakota to the east. His image was used by young men to assist them in courtship. They carved his graceful head and horns onto flutes and pipes or made leather elk cutouts as love charms. A man who dreamed of elk could become a member of the Elk Dreamers Society. According to ethnologist Clark Wissler, the "dreamers of the elk are supposed to be privileged to steal women" (Wissler 1912, p. 87). Like the mountain cats, these animals are drawn in profile. The elk's light neck ruff is delicately indicated through a series of parallel lines.

Plains artists incorporated the newly liberated Spanish horse into a cultural and spiritual world view by adorning it—painting spirit patterns on its flanks for warfare, tying its tail, creating beaded bridles and other equine ornaments. They also used art symbolically to obtain horses—carving miniature horses as "wishes" or drawing horses at pictograph sites.

Every artist "borrows" what seems to "fit." Navajo weavers responded to the introduction of aniline dyes by creating "eye dazzler" patterns with the new color palette. Plains quill workers incorporated glass beads and developed flexible patterns based on the dot as an analog to the line. Some scholars think nineteenth-century pictograph artists were influenced by the realist traditions of visiting painters such as George Catlin, Karl Bodmer, and Paul Kane. Depiction of equestrian figures became less stylized after contact with these artists. Influence goes the other way, of course—twentieth-century "modern" art would not exist as it is without the impact of Indian, African, and Oceanic art.

Plains people moved around; many early observers noticed a sort of shorthand visual language created along hunting, trade, and warfare routes. John Nicollet, traveling in the 1830s, stated, "They use this figurative language strictly for their needs as they travel or hunt or wage war in order to make known their whereabouts and the events they witnessed, to show where they came from, where they are heading, and what they saw, etc. They mark all these things at the confluences of rivers, on lake shores, on portage trails, always in the most conspicuous places" (Bray 1970, p. 266).

Scholar David W. Penny thinks some horse images are "a prayer for blessings, which included ownership of horses." Others are picture narratives in which the horse plays a role. This horse could be a wish. Pecked tenderly into a rock face in southeastern Colorado, it is superimposed over earlier images that look like tally marks or counting.

PUBLIC SITES

Asterisk denotes a site discussed or illustrated in the previous section.

Look for additional listings for South Texas and Colorado in *Southwest* section, Oklahoma under *Mississippi River,* Idaho in section on *California, the Great Basin, and the Plateau.*

ALBERTA (Canada)
Writing-on-Stone Provincial Park*
Over 700 rock drawings incised on eroded boulders and cliffs. The park is located 22 miles east of the town of Milk River, off Highway 501.

COLORADO
Purgatoire River Petroglyphs*
Petroglyphs along canyon walls of the Purgatoire River. Located in the Cedar Breaks region off Highways 101 and 109.

Vogel Canyon Petroglyphs
Rock drawings created over a thousand-year period embellish cliffs in the Comanche Grasslands. Drive on Highway 109, 12 miles south of LaJunta. Take David Canyon Road for 1.5 miles to a marker, then left onto Grand Road for 2 miles to a parking area and foot trail.

IDAHO
Jaguar Cave/ Indian Head Canyon*
Pictographs made by ancestral Shoshone, located near Challis in the Birch Creek Valley. There are also many pictograph sites in nearby Big Springs canyon area, located above the Big Lost River Valley near Challis.

KANSAS
Ellsworth County Historical Society/Hodgden House Museum
Replicas of petroglyphs of central Kansas are found in the museum on Main Street in Ellsworth.

MISSOURI
Thousand Hills State Park
Petroglyphs protected by contemporary shelter. The drawings are related to Mississippian cultures. Follow Route 6, 3 miles west of Kirksville, then south 2 miles on Missouri 157 to the park.

Washington State Park
Hundreds of rock drawings made between the eleventh and seventeenth centuries, and a Mound Builder site. The park is located 15 miles south of DeSoto on Missouri 21.

MONTANA
Pictograph Caves State Park
Red, black, and white pictographs made during 10,000 years of habitation. This National Historic Landmark is located 7 miles southeast of Billings off Interstate 90 at the Lockwood Exit.

Pompey's Pillar National Historic Landmark
A dramatic sandstone pillar engraved with petroglyphs and an additional 1806 signature by William Clark. Drive 28 miles east of Billings to the Pompey Pillar exit, then one mile north on Route 312.

NORTH DAKOTA

Writing Rock State Historic Site
Thunderbird images on glacial boulders are located on County Road north from Grenora on North Dakota 50.

SASKATCHEWAN (Canada)

Herschel Petroglyphs
Rock carvings on 2 limestone boulders 2.5 kilometers west of Herschel.

Indian Rock Art
Red pictographs at several sites in the Churchill River system. Take a boat for viewing near Pelican Narrows at Medicine Rapids, Larocque Lake, and other places along the Churchill River.

St. Victor's Petroglyphs
Petroglyphs on stone outcroppings above the town of St. Victor's. Climb a long stairway from St. Victor's to Petroglyphs Historic Park.

SOUTH DAKOTA

Craven Canyon
Numerous petroglyphs inscribed into sandstone walls of Red Canyon, located about 12 miles north of Edgemont.

Ludlow Cave*
The cave contains petroglyphs made by Sioux and earlier people who used this site. It is located west of Ludlow in the South Cave Hills.

TEXAS

Big Bend National Park
Pictographs near Hot Springs Nature Trail. Take Texas 385 off U.S. 90 in Marathon and drive 69 miles to the park headquarters.

Devil's River Natural Area
Many early pictographs throughout the region. Follow Highway 277, 45 miles north from Del Rio; turn onto Dolan's Creek Road and drive 22 miles to park headquarters.

Panther Cave*
Polychrome pictographs featuring panther deities and other supernaturals painted inside caves at the junction of the Rio Grande and Seminole Canyon. You must travel by boat 25 miles downstream from the Pecos River boat ramp to the Panther Cave dock, located within Amistad Recreation Area northwest of Comstock on U.S. 90.

WYOMING

Castle Gardens*
Numerous rock drawings, including many depicting shields. The site is located about 50 miles east of Saint Stevens Mission near the Wind River Reservation boundary.

Medicine Creek Cave
Petroglyphs depicting animals along box canyon walls. Located about 60 miles from Sundance near Devil's Tower; this site is on the Wyoming Geological Survey.

Medicine Lodge Archaeological Site
An interpretive trail leads to petroglyphs along red sandstone cliffs. Follow signs for 6 miles north on country road from Hyattville.

GREAT LAKES
AND THE NORTHEAST

We are entering the great northern forests, with their networks of vast lakes and bushy creeks. The colors are silver, black, green. People used forest products to make their art—birch bark scrolls, wooden paddles with etched mnemonic symbols, images carved into trees as signs and pecked onto rocks, often near the waterways that served as roads. This art could be "read" as songs or stories. The people along the Great Lakes and tributary rivers were Algonquians, Ojibwa, Ottawa, Potawatomi, Menominee, Winnebago, Sauk and Fox, Kickapoo, Miami, Illinois, Shawnee.

This pipe-smoker is painted in red against a granite boulder in East La Croix, Ontario. He is probably Ojibwa; his leggings could be ceremonial. The actual pipe was very likely red as well, carved from a stone artist George Catlin called steatite. After he managed to find the sacred quarry, the stone bore his name—catlinite.

Rock art sites are often associated with nesting birds, especially eagles and hawks, relatives of Thunderbird deity. Ojibwa elders described these sites to ethnologist Thor Conway. They called them *muzzinabikin*, or "markings on rock," and considered a cliff nest a sign of blessing for the drawings. Tobacco smoke is associated with birds as well. Its smoke flies to the sky deities. A pipe may be wrapped in bird-skin, blurring its identity as spirit messenger.

Ojibwa Dan Pine spoke about the red pigment: "Oh, that's the paint that doesn't scrub off. *Muskwa*. Red. Red is a spiritual color. . . . Red rock is used for pipestone. My people collected red paint. They saw it seeping out of the bank at Island Lake just like mud. . . . The spiritual people painted the rocks just like the spirits painted the animals' fur. The red paint has a blend of power that overcomes the evil power" (Conway 1993, pp. 42–44).

This horned turtle is incised into an outcropping of red quartzite at Jeffers Petroglyphs State Park in Minnesota. Some images at Jeffers date from 3000 B.C., but this turtle was probably pecked after the tenth century by an ancestor of the Sioux, whose early homes were near the Great Lakes.

Turtles symbolize the cosmos for many Native cultures. The Seneca tell a story about The Woman Who Fell from the Sky. Loon and Bittern spied her slowly falling from a hole in the sky into their lower water world. They devised a plan for her rescue and convinced Turtle to float on the surface. Cushioned by a flock of ducks, the woman was gently deposited on the back of the Great Turtle. While she slept, exhausted, Beaver, Otter, and Muskrat took turns retrieving bottom mud and creating land on Turtle's carapace. The woman woke on earth.

Lakota Sioux women bead tiny turtle amulets and place a daughter's umbilical cord inside, literally tying her to Earth. The U-shaped yoke pattern of a traditional beaded Lakota dress is called "turtle-by-the-shore." Some cultures see the four legs of the turtle as the four directions, another earth symbol.

And today? The turtle, like the frog, occupies both land and water. Both are sensitive to the thinning of the ozone layer of our atmosphere; it weakens their eggs. The turtle points out directions for a future we could avert by paying attention to the signs.

The word "moose" is derived from the Algonquian *mooswa* or *moos*. It's at home here, the dominant animal of the northern forests. You don't readily see a moose; it's solitary. In winter, a few might shelter together and feed on tree bark; in summer, you could encounter a cow and calf. I once saw five moose standing quietly by the tracks as the train I was riding twisted through the Canadian Rockies toward Quebec. A friend tells another story. A group of artists and musicians were living in the Maine woods, working with the Bread and Puppet Theater. They created homemade versions of Indonesian gamelan instruments out of saw blades and were performing a night concert in a clearing. Into the campfire light stepped a bull moose. The audience hushed, the moose stared, paused, then returned silently to the woods.

Woodlands people used this same principle to hunt moose, reproducing the mating sounds of a cow with a birch bark horn or scraping a moose shoulder bone against a tree to imitate the scratching antlers of a bull in rut. The same intimacy shows in this pictograph. When people depend on an animal for sustenance, they observe carefully. They also venerate that animal. This bull moose from Hegman Lake in Minnesota is painted with tender realism. The standing figure has the distorted proportions of a supernatural. Above are tiny canoes. In one the passenger is a crane.

The moose cow and calf on the next page are painted on a lichen-spotted rock at Darky Lake, Quetico Provincial Park, Ontario. The spirit moose on page 121 is near Basswood River, Boundary Waters Canoe Area Wilderness, Minnesota. Painted in profile, he is smoking a ceremonial pipe. All three pictographs are red; the artists were probably Ojibwa.

This is a third-generation drawing from incised Seneca images copied by a French missionary in 1664. The originals were carved into birch bark, perhaps on the living tree. Several drawing conventions are merged here.

The idea of copying a painting is a familiar concept. Plains artists would "renew" a vision tipi when the original wore out by repainting the same image onto a new covering. Some Great Lakes pictographs have been overpainted; scientists from the Canadian Conservation Institute who tested paint samples with an electron microscope discovered multiple layers of color washes. Vision seekers in the Columbia Plateau and artists in the Southwest routinely added new drawings to pictograph panels, sometimes pecking or painting over earlier ones.

Is the act of drawing at specific sites more important than the previous image? Is the site the source of power? Or does the image itself hold a power that can be amplified by repainting, erasing, pecking? European "masterpieces" are frequently repainted and "restored." The act of conservation reaffirms the power of the particular work of art. It makes the art seem immutable to change.

This deer is an Iroquois clan symbol. The Seneca were one of the original Five Nations of the Iroquois Confederacy (which included Mohawk, Oneida, Onondaga, and Cayuga), occupants of the regions near the Saint Lawrence River and traditional enemies of the Great Lakes Algonquians. It is no accident that Deer holds a tomahawk. The original drawings made a narrative. Most likely, they were carved into a tree so passersby could learn the news they conveyed.

Here is Thunderbird, Animkeeg, in a dress suit, one of the deeply indented petroglyphs carved into marble at Teaching Rock, Petroglyphs Provincial Park, in Peterborough, Ontario, a site sacred to the contemporary Ojibwa Anishinabe Nation. Thunderbird is usually painted with his face in profile, the wings outstretched, sometimes with a heartline, sometimes with radiating spirit waves. In this image the line between bird and human is blurred; the wings could almost be elongated arms. But the wings are the thunder source—Aminkeeg generates storms by beating his wings. His cosmic rival, the underwater panther Michipeshu, stirs up storms with its tail. The two are in epic struggle, sky force against underwater.

The Brule Sioux call Thunderbird Wakinyan. The great cat is Unkthei. When he was a boy, Sioux elder John (Fire) Lame Deer was out looking for horses and got caught in the Badlands during a torrential nighttime storm—thunderclaps, hail, the smell of lightning. In terror he clung to a canyon ridge. "But I felt the presence of the Wakinyan, heard them calling me through the thunder: 'Don't be afraid! Hold on! You'll be all right!' At last the storm ended, and finally dawn came. Then I saw that I was straddling a long row of petrified bones, the biggest I have ever seen. I had been moving along the spine of the Great Unkthei . . ." (Erdoes 1984, p. 222).

Rock images can depict both the unseen and the seen. When the first thunder sounds in the spring here in New Mexico, the snakes emerge from their holes. Ojibwa Dan Pine told Thor Conway that vision questing started in the spring so one could hear "Thunder's cry." Nineteenth-century ethnologist William J. Hoffman described the Menominee's Thunder spirits—the powerful Manitous. "The latter consisted of eagles or hawks, known as thunderers, *a-na-maq-ki*, chief of which is the invisible thunder, though represented by the *k'ne-u*, the golden eagle" (Hoffman 1890, p. 243).

There's a bird petroglyph near my house, pecked high on a cliff. I spotted it while watching a hawk soar.

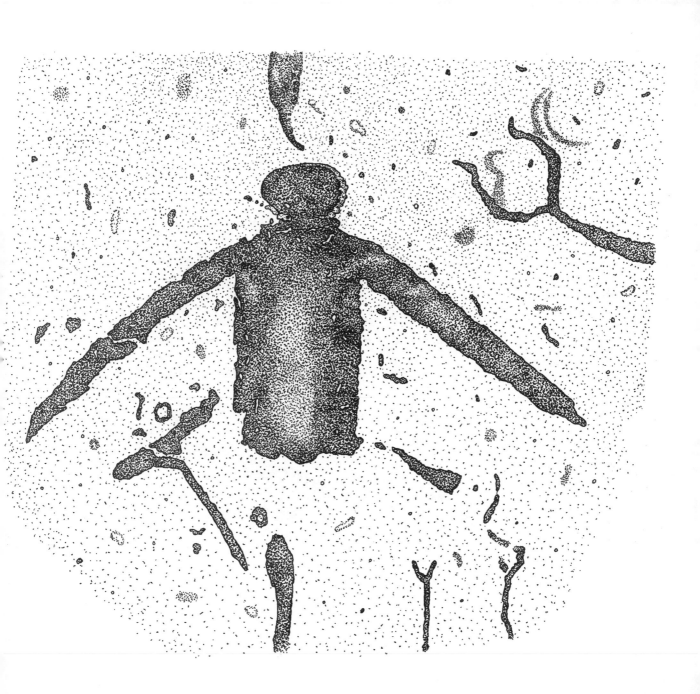

No one knows exactly who painted this famous red pictograph of the underwater panther Michipeshu at Agawa Rock, Lake Superior Provincial Park in Ontario. It is one of seventeen pictograph panels painted near the base of the pink granite cliffs with the lake lapping nearby. Most are individual visions painted by shamans; some images, such as this underwater panther, have been layered with successive paintings. Two of the artists are known. Nineteenth-century anthropologist Henry Rowe Schoolcraft interviewed Ojibwa artist-shaman Shingwauk or "The White Pine" and also named a seventeenth-century leader named Myeengun or "The Wolf." Others attribute some paintings to "the little wild men." Chief Norma Fox of the Cockburn Island Ojibwa described these supernaturals. "The pygmies or wild men can capture and kill the Chignebikoog (Giant Snakes) and use the giant serpent's blood to paint on the cliffs" (Conway 1990, p. 29). Others associate the big snakes with copper, either their flesh is copper or the snakes buried copper, gold, and silver under the earth, like the dragon who hoards gold.

Michipeshu is painted with two of these giant reptiles flanked by people in a canoe. The canoe might help create the illusion of water. The great panther lives under Lake Superior.

More panthers are shown on the next two pages. Both are Winnebago. The petroglyph on page 128 is from northeastern Nebraska. The Great Cat is accompanied by a horned shaman; she is spiny like the Agawa Rock image, but the tail is reversed. The twin panthers on page 129 are also accompanied by a great snake and other creatures, a naturalistic deer and what appear to be buffalo. These figures are incised onto an antler war club, collected in 1839 at Fort Winnebago; the animals probably represent the vision helpers of the warrior. And are weapons appropriate here? At the base of Agawa Rock, archaeologists have found many layers of arrowheads. Some interpret these weapons as offerings to the paintings, shot at a safe distance from the sacred.

These drawings were incised onto a flat wooden paddle by a Potawatomi healer as a memory aide in preserving herbal recipes and curing rituals. It's called a prescription stick and was made in Mayetta, Kansas, around 1860. Each section between the vertical lines is a single herbal formula; I have drawn four recipes. The images represent specific plants, but they are not naturalistic. You can't take this drawing into the fields and identify the herbs.

Midewiwin priests used a similar drawing system to depict the complex ritual songs and dances of the Great Lakes religion, a highly stylized visual convention that could be "read" only by specialists. An initiate would undergo a long period of training in order to interpret the symbols and gain the right to sing the songs encoded in the pictographs.

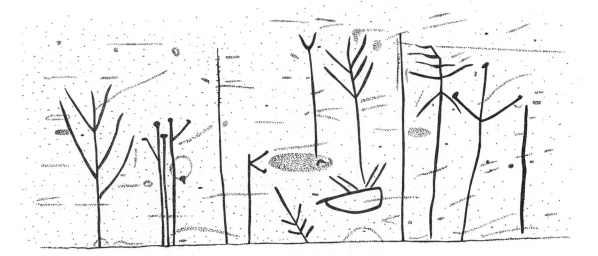

Ethnologist W. J. Hoffman studied with a Mide priest at Mille Lacs, Minnesota, in the nineteenth century. He quoted the lyrics on one sequence of images. "My arm is almost pulled out from digging medicine. It is full of medicine/Almost crying because the medicine is lost/Yes there is much medicine you may cry for/Yes I see there is plenty of it/Rest" (Penny 1992, p. 63).

We regularly adorn our bodies with visual symbols printed on shirts or hats. An archeologist of the twenty-third century would puzzle over the proliferation of the Nike logo for instance, or the golden arches of McDonalds. Neither bears any resemblance to a hamburger or a pair of sneakers, yet we are all initiates in this contemporary visual language.

The drawings on Teaching Rock, Petroglyphs Provincial Park, in Peterborough, Ontario, were pecked into the undulating marble bedrock. A spring trickles beneath the rock and bubbles up into the crevices to flow like a viscous lubricant over this extraordinary artwork. The images were probably made 500 to 1,000 years ago, most likely over a long period. Ojibwa artists left their hammerstones stored in the rock crevices. The images were deeply indented, then colored with dark pigment to contrast with the light marble, giving the effect of highly patterned silhouettes.

Formerly you came upon this site sheltered in a forest, but the influx of visitors and the changes in the woods caused the drawings to deteriorate. They were colored with crayon, possibly similar to the grease and pigment paints of the Pecos River artists in Texas. Algae began to grow. Now the crayon has been removed with dry air abrasion and the embellished bedrock enclosed inside a glass building. You walk along a catwalk and look down on the images.

I think the viewer was always meant to move around and over the drawings. They change with your vantage point. The great crane on the top, reversed, looks like a kneeling figure with upraised arms. Is this intentional, creating a permeable barrier between human and crane? We listen to Ojibwa elder Fred Pine: "I got this little bird with long legs inside me. He walks around very proud. He is a smart bird. He traveled a long ways too. This bird is very quick. That's what I carry. N'Dodem. My totem. Gee-Sheesh-Kinay. Sand piper" (Conway 1990, p. 19).

Most of the animals in this section are reptiles and amphibians—a turtle with eggs, snakes, lizards with heads that seem to indicate gender, snails, human-snake figures. The animal below the crane crosses between human and insect—a literal walking stick. We are in the fecund stream bed. The giant arrowhead is the only "manufactured" object in the frieze.

PUBLIC SITES

Asterisk denotes a site discussed or illustrated in the previous section.

The list below includes more than pictograph sites. I've named places with animal-shaped earthworks plus some giant intaglio images as part of the national "gallery" of outdoor artworks. I've also included sites related to the Algonquians and Iroquoians of the populous Northeast/Great Lakes woodlands. The Eastern Algonquians, settled along the Atlantic coast, include Micmac, Malecite, Delaware or Lenni-Lenape, Passamaquoddy, Eastern Abenaki, Nanticote, Powhatan, Pequot, Penobscot, Wampanoag, Narraganset, Massachuset. Counted among Iroquoians near the Susquehanna and Saint Lawrence Rivers are Mahican, Mohegan, Tuscarora, Huron, Erie, and Susquehannock.

INDIANA

Mounds State Park

Earthworks created by the Adena culture, some with astronomical alignments. The park is located 4 miles east of Anderson on Indiana 232.

IOWA

Effigy Mounds National Monument

Almost 200 mounds built over 1,500 years, some in the shapes of bears or birds. Drive 3 miles north of Marquette on Iowa 76.

Turkey River Mounds

Forty-five mounds built 2,000 years ago at the confluence of the Turkey and Mississippi Rivers, located 4 miles from Guttenberg on U.S. 52.

KENTUCKY

Adena Park

Circular earthwork built by Adena people. Drive 8 miles from Lexington on U.S. 27 to Old Ironworks Road, then onto Mount Horeb Pike. The park is on North Elkhorn Creek.

MANITOBA (Canada)

Bannock Point Petroform Site
(also called *Ojibwa Boulder Mosaic)*

Numerous giant "petroforms," or images outlined with rocks. The images are located within Whiteshell Provincial Park about 20 miles west of Manitoba on Trans-Canada Highway 1 at the Manitoba-Ontario border on Manitoba 44.

MASSACHUSETTS

Dighton Rock State Park

A 40-ton boulder with inscriptions made either by Indians or by Cotton Mather or other settlers. The park is in the town of Assonet near Fall River.

MICHIGAN

Sanilac Petroglyphs State Park

Numerous images pecked into a sandstone outcropping, protected by a contemporary shelter. The park is located in Sanilac County's Greenleaf Township near the junction of Bay City–Forestville Road and Germania Road, 4 miles east of Michigan 53.

MINNESOTA

Jeffers Petroglyphs State Park*

More than 2,000 rock drawings on a sloping outcropping of red quartzite, dating from 3000 B.C. to the eighteenth century. Jeffers is located near Bingham Lake off U.S. 71. Take County Road 10 east 3 miles, then County Road 2 south one mile.

NEW JERSEY

Seaton Hall University, Archaeological Research Center and Museum

The museum contains a boulder from New Jersey incised with petroglyphs. Go to Fahy Hall on South Orange Avenue in South Orange.

NEW YORK

American Museum of Natural History

Extraordinary art collection from many Native American cultures. Take the subway to Central Park West and 79th Street, New York City.

NOVA SCOTIA

Petroglyphs

Rock art in various locations near Lake Kidgemakooge.

OHIO

Cincinnati Art Museum

The so-called Adena tablets are housed here, incised onto slabs. The museum is in Eden Park, Cincinnati.

Inscription Rock

Large boulder covered with rock drawings made from the eleventh to the seventeenth centuries. The site is located on Kelley's Island in Lake Erie, north of Sandusky.

Leo Petroglyph

Many images on a stone slab a little northwest of Leo.

Serpent Mound State Memorial

A huge earthwork snake nearly one-quarter mile in length. It is located on Ohio 73, 4 miles northwest of Locust Grove.

ONTARIO (Canada)

Agawa Rock Pictographs*

Seventeen panels of red pictographs painted by Ojibwa shamans. The pictographs are in Lake Superior Park near Agawa Bay Campground. There is a marked trail off Highway 17.

Petroglyphs Provincial Park*

Intricately pecked drawings on a large boulder inside a protective structure. The site is sacred to the Ojibwa Anishinabe Nation. The park is located northeast of Peterborough about 11 kilometers from Highway 28.

Serpent Mound Provincial Park

A large snake effigy mound on the north shore of Rice Lake near Peterborough.

WISCONSIN

Devil's Lake State Park

Earthworks in the shapes of animals, including a bear, a lynx, and a bird. Drive 3 miles south of Baraboo on Wisconsin 123.

High Cliff State Park

Effigy mounds in the shapes of lizards and birds. The park is located 10 miles east of Menasha on Wisconsin 114.

Lizard Mound County Park

Thirty-one effigy mounds of various animals and geometric shapes, including birds, lizards, and panthers. Drive 4 miles northeast from West Bend on Wisconsin 114 to County Trunk A, then one mile to the marker.

Man Mound Park

A large earthwork in the shape of a person located near Baraboo off County Trunk T.

Panther Intaglio

A large deeply inset panther intaglio west of Fort Atkinson on Wisconsin 106.

Roche-a-Cri State Park

Petroglyphs obscured by modern graffiti are incised into a mound. Drive one mile north of Friendship on Wisconsin 13.

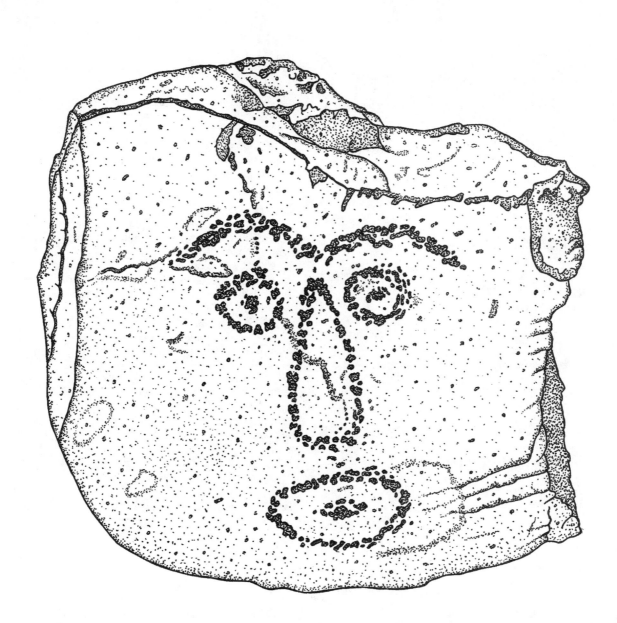

NORTHWEST COAST, ARCTIC, AND SUBARCTIC

Y ou didn't need to farm. The Northwest Coast was a watery cornucopia, supplying 100 inches of yearly rain, five different kinds of salmon; halibut, cod, smelt, herring, candlefish, clams, mollusks, and seaweed; plus edible sea mammals such as whale, porpoise, seal, sea lion, otter. You stepped off the beach into the cedar forests for wood, bark, wild berries, deer. Look along the beach when the tides recede. On the boulders or steep cliffs fronting the water you can see incised drawings addressed to these creatures, the providers of bounty.

This boulder is a kind of mask—found by chance along the west shore of Agate Passage near Bremerton, Oregon. A man named William Lane was working to restore the beach. He picked up this stone to add to his bulkhead and uncovered a face.

Scholar D. Leechman wrote in 1952 about a similar mask. He was canoeing with an Indian friend and they paused on a beach at Agate Passage, waiting for the tides to change. His friend started pecking a face onto a boulder with a pebble. "I asked him if he had made this face and he answered that he had carved this one and some of the others and his father had done the rest ... merely to pass the time while waiting for the tide to change" (Hill 1978, p. 21).

What did Mr. Lane find? A mere doodle or a sketch from a faded tradition that held a different value in an earlier period? Squaxin parents used to warn their children to avoid walking in front of the petroglyphs around Puget Sound. Does this boulder hold the same power? Collectors trade the sketches Picasso doodled on his dinner napkins. In an earlier period, Picasso could have been employed as a fresco painter in a cathedral and the doodler on the beach would have been fasting in an icy tide before rendering his rock drawing.

There were numerous cultures stretched along the northwest coast from California to Alaska. Many still occupy their ancestral regions. To the south were Makah, Salish, Chemakum, Chinook, Tillamook, Quinault. Kwakiutl and Nootka lived around Vancouver Island and Alert Bay. Further north were Tlingit, Haida, Tsimshian, Bella Coola. People worked in the warm months, setting up seasonal camps for fishing or berry picking or hunting. The winter was a time for creativity and staying at home. You can see the results in early photos of the region—intricate variations of house design, painting, carved totems, a great variety of masks and elaborate ceremonial costumes, complex religious theater and dance, drawings pecked into surface rocks or along coastal boulders.

These women are appropriately placed next to a rock formation that resembles a vulva. The Latin origin of the word internalizes the organ, "womb, covering." This petroglyph multiplies it with female symbols as hands, headdress, earrings; the smaller figure is all vulva. The women are joyous. Their hands are upraised like the southwestern Mother deities. They seem to be singing or calling. The artists may have been singing too. Ethnologist T. F. McIllwraith heard this Bella Coola story about making petroglyphs. They were pecked by "leaders" a long time ago. "They picked out the rock in time to the music forming in their minds" (Hill 1978, p. 22).

These figures were incised into a sheer cliff near Ozette, an old Makah whaling village at Cape Alava on the Washington coast. Ozette was buried in a mud slide 450 years ago; six preserved plank houses and their contents have recently been excavated. The petroglyphs are about three miles away. The site mimics procreation. The water laps at the cliff and seeps into the fissures near the drawings. Contemporary people see the metaphor as easily as the ancients. The place is called Wedding Rocks. Are the Mothers incised here to promote aquatic fertility? Whales pass closer to land near Ozette than anywhere along the coast.

Some writers call this intaglio carving "man-who-fell-from-the-sky." It is deeply indented into a boulder at Prince Rupert Harbour in British Columbia. It could be contemporary art, a mud-impressed "silhouette" by Ana Mendieta. The figure is horizontal, like the two petroglyphs on the following pages. The rock is pocked with natural "basins" that hold water— a northwestern "tank rain" site. Even on this wet coast, rain matters. People from Puget Sound would ritually shake the rock incised with a thunderbird at Eneti when the salmon were slow returning upstream. Salmon need storms to raise the water level before they can enter the creeks to spawn. Here is a different kind of symbolic food cultivation.

But is this intaglio related to rain? I think the figure is a woman, partly because of the rock crevices that surround her. She is masked but her body is naturalistic. Would one lie inside the image, the way a Navajo might place her hands over incised ones in prayer? The artist could be Tshimshian.

The drawings on the next pages also merge naturalism and artifice. The idiosyncratic figure on page 142 was uncovered when a road was plowed for a power line about two miles from Nanaimo Petroglyph Park on Vancouver Island. It was under a thick layer of moss, pecked into bedrock on Harewood Plain. It is almost life-size, about five feet long. Some writers call this image a hermaphrodite. Beth Hill thinks the skewed eyes could indicate visionary power. The figure might have been drawn by an initiate for a secret society. Anthropologist C. F. Newcombe describes the training of initiates "during which they sometimes had to illustrate . . . the spirits with which they held communion" (Hill 1978, p. 37).

The man on page 143 is pecked into a creek bed at Ford Creek on Hornby Island, his legs flexed and arms raised in a traditional dance pose. This is clearly a human wearing a mask. Who or what is being personified?

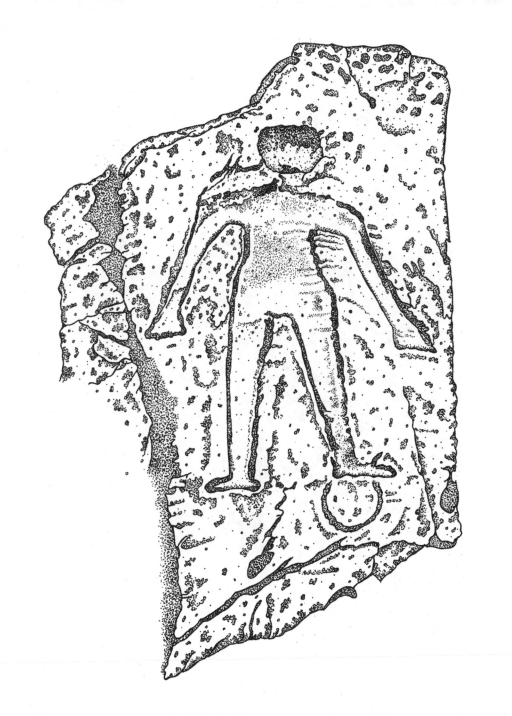

The dragon-like creature above is incised into the same rock field as the duck dancer across from the title page. It emerged from a thick covering of dirt in 1969 when a driveway was plowed near the Nanaimo River in Vancouver. The depth of soil is estimated at a thousand years. It may be a "sea-wolf" or "Sea-Grisly"—the Haida call him Wasgo. Charles Edensaw drew a detailed version of Wasgo for ethnologist Franz Boas in 1927 and described him as part wolf, part killer whale.

There are many versions of these "dragons." The Kwakiutl Sisiutl is a double-faced serpent with a snout like the sea snakes (above) at Nanaimo Petroglyph Park. Sisiutl can transform himself from sky into lightning, from fish into a canoe. Like Quetzalcoatl, he can be both bird and reptile. A sailor on the Columbia witnessed a monstrous reptile emerging from the water near Clayoquot in 1791. "The Indians knew all about it and described it as a long creature with a huge mouth and teeth; in every other respect like a serpent. They called it Haietlik and said it was very scarce" (Hill 1978, p. 121).

My grandfather used to say, "I saw a scary man, toes in front and heels behind." His prosaic version of the boogie man made us children run inside. The goblin was originally "Booger" man, one of the masked Cherokee dancers from the Booger Dance. It originated in the sixteenth century as a burlesque reenactment of the Hernando de Soto invasion of Florida—a way to ritualize loss.

Disturbing images are incised into the bedrock at Thorsen Creek. Some believe that the big-eyed creature is a slave sacrificed at a *potlatch* or an executed prisoner. The bird has eyes like the handles of scissors and the goggle-eyed person is reduced to a monstrous face.

Some elites from the more stratified northern cultures—Haida, Kwakiutl, Tsimshian, and Tlingit—owned slaves or war captives. Slaves could be players in the winter ceremonial, often called a *potlatch,* a Chinook term meaning "to give." A wealthy person might hold a *potlatch* to bestow a title or initiate a relative into a secret society, giving him the rights to use the sacred songs and dances passed down in a family. The host would invite guests to several days of feasting and ritual performances. One of these dances was the *hamatsa,* or cannibal dance—the "wild man" theatrically ate flesh or committed murder. Later, the "victim" might emerge whole. It was a sleight-of-hand sacrifice. Is this petroglyph a record of the "place where the slave had been eaten" on the beach, as a witness from the Hudson's Bay Company told ethnologist Franz Boas? Or is it a layered depiction of cannibalism with rebirth the emerging theme?

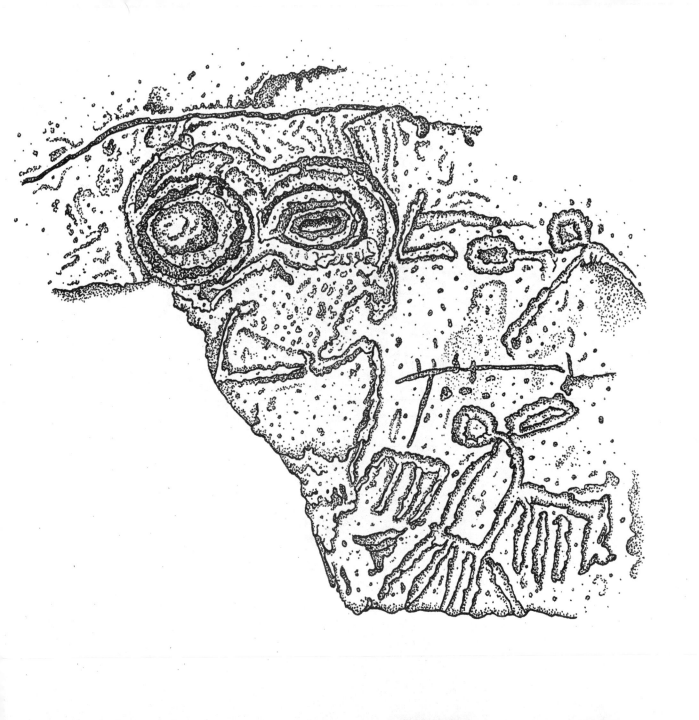

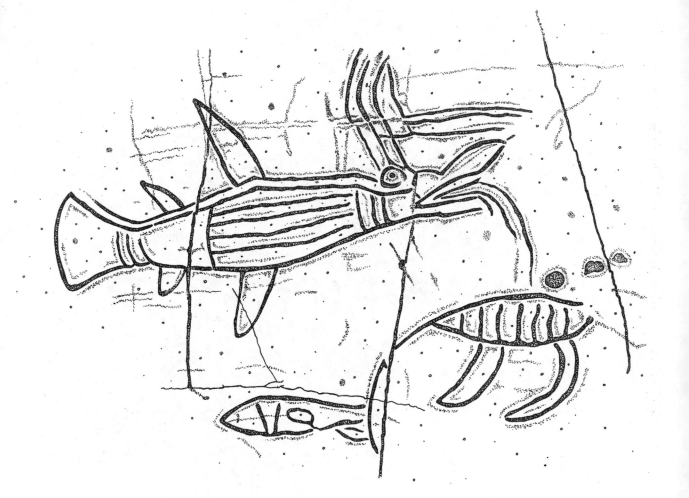

The petroglyphs at Sproat Lake on Vancouver Island, British Columbia, are periodically concealed. You can view them in warm months from a platform floating in the lake; in winter they are underwater. They were placed to emerge and submerge with the tides, alternately visible to humans and fish. Nootka shamans may have incised these creatures while fasting in the icy water. The dog-faced one drawn here has fins and swims above a fish. It could be the "sea-snake," Haietlik, described earlier. Thunderbird could kill a whale by hurling Haietlik like a harpoon.

The coastal people believed that salmon were people who lived in a village under the sea. Each year, the Salmon People would conceal themselves as fish and migrate upstream to sacrifice their flesh for humans. People saved the bones after eating and returned them to the sea so the Salmon People could be reborn. If the salmon didn't return, a Nootka shaman would put an image of a fish into the water at their usual migration place. Franz Boas wrote in 1890: "This ceremony, accompanied by a prayer to the fish to come, will cause them to arrive at once."

The skeletal salmon on the following pages were incised into a boulder with natural rippling that imitated waves. A bird is merged with one of the fish. This boulder was at Jack Point, a promontory jutting into Nanaimo Harbour. If the fish run was late, the pecked images would be painted in red ochre. A story associated with the drawings is that a dog salmon ran off with a chief's daughter. You could see the couple each year returning, leaping out of the water. A pair of fish would be painted in red ochre and tufted with down before the first roasted salmon could be eaten. You can now visit this boulder in front of the Nanaimo City Museum, detached from its ritual context.

The fish on page 151 is a finely drawn flounder swimming above a skeletized sea-snake on horizontal bedrock near Chase River, Petroglyph Park, Nanaimo.

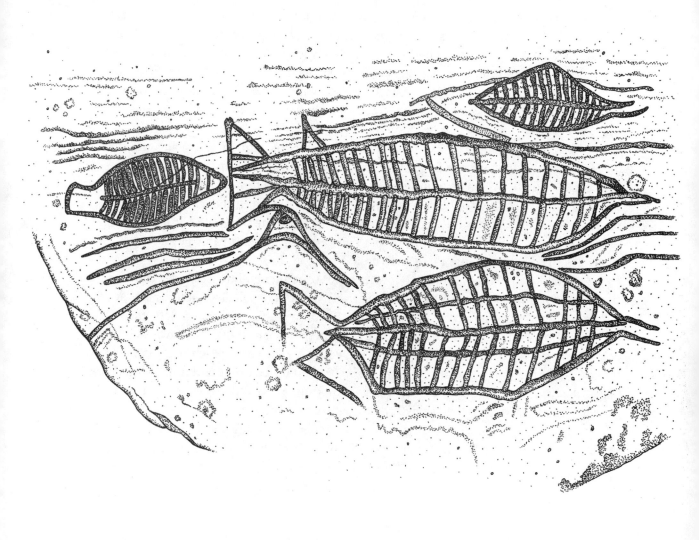

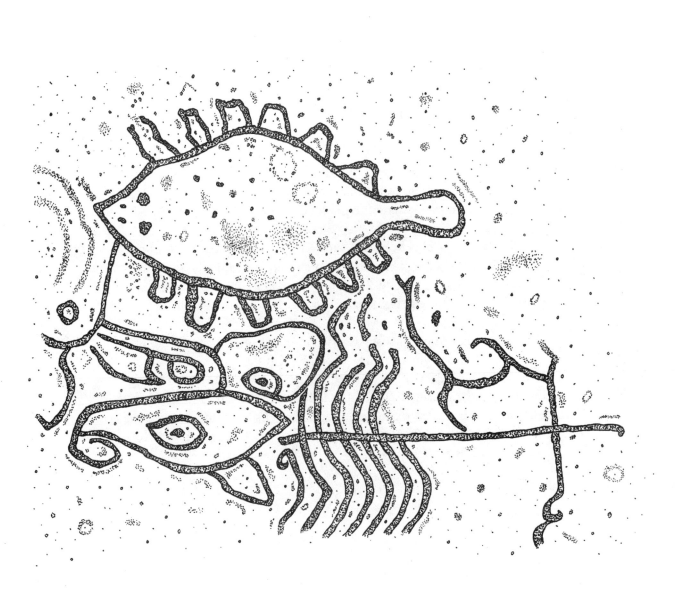

Northwest Coast petroglyphs don't seem to be layered or repainted like those in many other sites around the country. They are not always pecked with hammerstones. Some are rubbed using sticks and beach sand. Many are drawn in thick smooth lines, like this composite animal face. It is incised among a group of drawings in the granite bedrock of Port Neville at a place called Robber's Knob, an inlet sheltered from the winds of the Johnstone Strait. The images, which were probably made by Salish artists, are visible at low tide. There are many simplified human faces pecked nearby, but only this single animal mask. Its horns are those of the pronghorn.

The Northwest Coast has a rich tradition of masks. A Kwakiutl dancer might lower his animal face, pull hidden strings and reveal the human mask inside. On the Bering Strait, an Inuit might see an animal reveal its human form. A Nelson Island hunter, visited by a wolf, described the encounter. "After doing something around its head/and doing something in its mouth/when it faced him/it became this way/taking its hood off" (Fitzhugh 1988, p. 259).

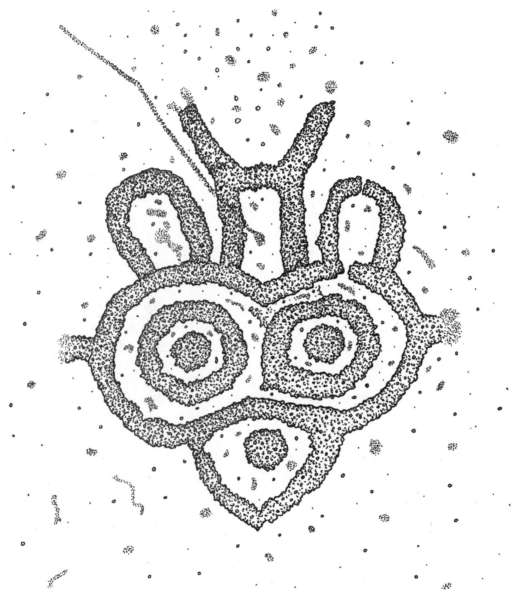

Migratory birds and waterfowl pass along the coast, which is part of the Pacific Flyway. This bird is hard to identify. It might be a curlew but the little creature in its beak isn't a normal avian. The rock drawings seem to merge naturalism with the eccentric detail of a dreamed image. A Salish shaman may have pecked this drawing into a round boulder on the beach at Cape Mudge. It's visible at low tide. Some scholars think the high cliff nearby was used by shamans for vision quests.

There are more birds on the following pages. The puffin on page 156 holds a rather obvious allusion to vision, a giant eye. This eye may be a reference to the puffin beak rattles used by Tlingit, Koniag, and Chugach shamans. The puffins are carved into bedrock granite near a lighthouse at Yellow Rock on the south end of Denman Island. The rocks here are embellished with forms of every kind—whales, sun, stars, supernaturals, birds, mammals. There used to be more drawings. Some were sacrificed to the construction of the lighthouse. The whole might have given a picture record of the bounty that sustained Northwest Coast cultures until the eighteenth-century fur trade depleted the natural resources. The antlered animal on page 157 has a puffin's beak and a bird-like tail, carved on sandstone at Nanaimo Petroglyph Park in Vancouver.

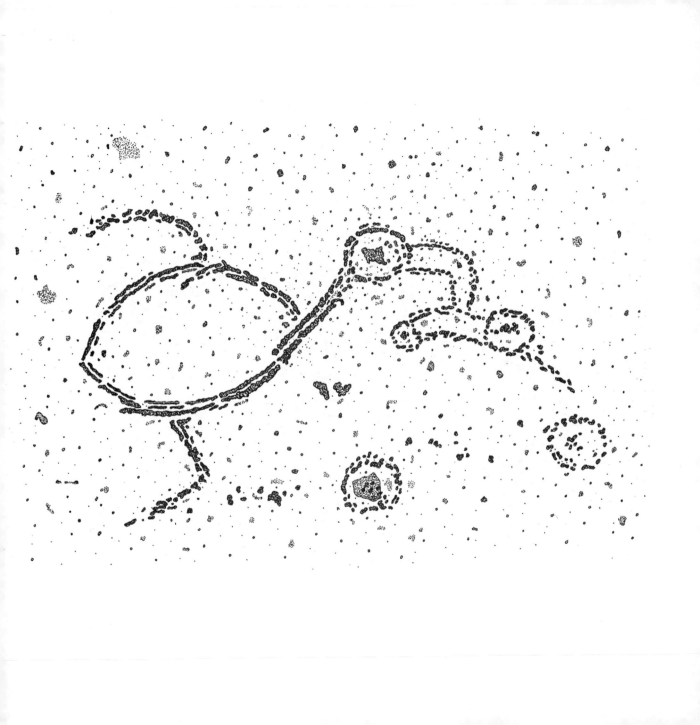

Through most of the year, these skeletized spirits are literally inside a major salmon river, the Skeena River on Ringbolt Island, British Columbia. You can view them by boating down Kitselas Canyon during April when the river is low, but you need first to obtain permission from the Kitselas Band on Ringbolt Island. They were probably pecked at great peril by Gitskan Tsimshian shamans. The petroglyphs are incised along sloping rocks above a swift current. You don't see these images by chance.

The drawings may mark a site that was already a sacred place. Garrick Mallery described the Sproat Lake petroglyphs in 1889. "According to their legend, the rock on which it was carved was once the house of Kwotiath. Kwotiath is the wandering divinity in Nootka mythology and corresponds approximately to the raven of the Tlingit and Haida" (Mallery 1972, Vol. I, p. 44). The artists selected a site associated with spirit birds, like the roosting places chosen for Great Lakes pictographs.

The figures here are not avian, though their skeletized bodies are ethereal. They seem to be placed to address underwater deities like the salmon and sea-grizzly at Jack Point or Sproat Lake. But these images are not the deities. The shaman has a staff and the dancing bears are holding a rope. Has the shaman descended into the swift currents with his medicine animals? His active skeleton could indicate a magical death and rebirth. Does this depict an actual ceremony?

Wood is scarce in the snowy Arctic. These drawings honoring food animals were carefully incised on a Bering Sea bentwood bowl, and on the next page, a wooden spoon. Artists are often "led" by their materials. Auguste Rodin felt he was pulling the figure out of the marble block as he carved. Georgia O'Keeffe felt like eating the colors as they emerged from the tube. The word "medium" is defined first as "middle," then as an "agency for transmitting energy," and "a means of communication." The Yupik artist who engraved the bowl was acting within all these word definitions. He was probably a hunter and incised the three caribou to honor the soul of the animals, the utility of the bowl, and his connection to the caribou in being allowed to kill them. Joe Friday of Chevak described this relationship to materials: "We felt like all things were like us people, to the small animals like the mouse and the things like wood we liken to people as having a sense of awareness. The wood is glad to the person who is using it and the person using it is grateful to the wood for being there to be used" (Fitzhugh 1988, p. 257).

Animals willingly let themselves be killed by a worthy hunter. The hunter, in turn, respected the animal by careful treatment of its bones. Ethnologist Ann Fienup-Riordan described people's behavior toward food: "Great effort was made to remove every scrap of meat from the seal bones. If this was not done, the seals would perceive the bones as singing loudly, warning them not to give themselves to these careless people" (Fitzhugh 1988, p. 258). The caribou and seal are drawn as skeletal spirits who will be reborn through return of their bones.

Both bentwood engravings show the animal's bladder, the place where its soul resides, called *inua*. The hands that encircle the seal on page 162 are probably those of Tunghak, a deity for game animals. The seal image on page 163 embellishes a sealskin float painted by a Koniag Inuit hunter. Harpoons were attached to the floats. Hunting implements were traditionally adorned with images that would please the prey.

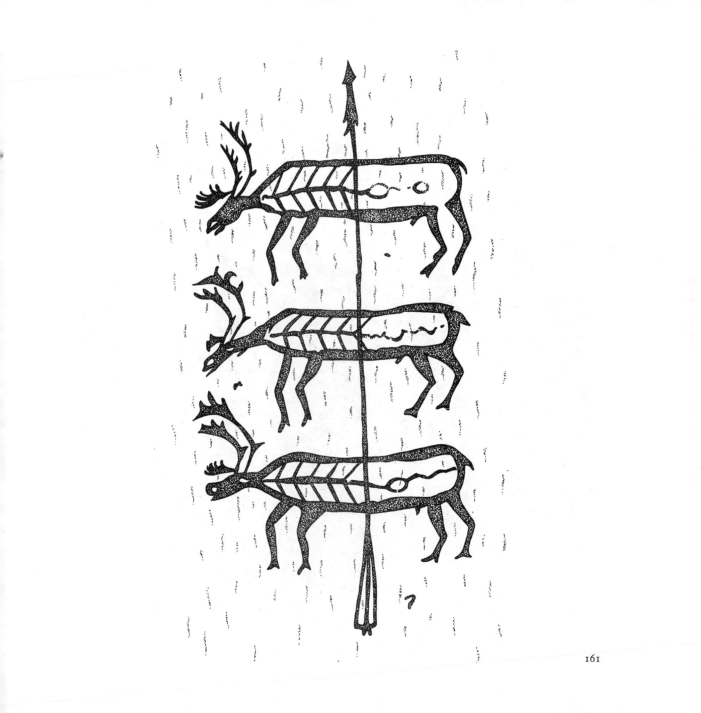

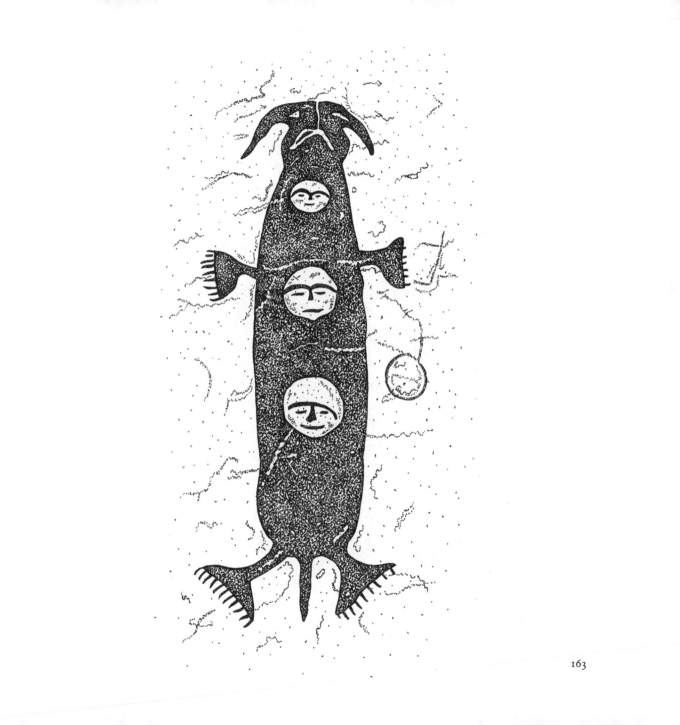

Traveling south from the Arctic tundra and the home of the Aleuts, Yupiks, and Inuits, we are back in the forests, with caribou, deer, moose, bear, and small animals such as beaver or otter who could be hunted for their fur or food. Cree, Athapaskan, Naskapi, Montagnais, Beothuk, Kutchin, Slavey, Dogrib are some of the cultures in this huge area of two million square miles. People lived by hunting. The animals provided food and clothing; their fur was traded for European goods. Women worked the hides into soft, fitted garments embellished with quilled patterns. Like the hunters to the north, subarctic hunters respected the spirits of their prey by honoring their bones. Beaver bones were returned to the creeks, the teeth of caribou, moose, and bear were cleaned and used as talismans, bear skulls were painted with red dots or stripes and placed in trees.

This Cree pictograph from northern Saskatchewan is painted in red, the spiritual color of Great Lakes art. This figure seems to be wearing animal-skin clothing. A tail dangles from each arm. It looks like a woman in a dress. But she's not drawn in natural proportions. She's probably a deity; some writers call her a Thunder Manitou. Or she could be one of those solitary prowler spirits that one meets in the night woods.

I end this journey with a face—an animal deeply incised in steatite by an Inuit artist on Qajartalik Island near Wakeham Bay, Quebec. I think this face is feline, but it shifts into human around the eyes. In a sense, all art masks or unmasks. We artists replicate. We take something that you might see naturally and mirror it in a different size and material. Or we make something that you can't see, make that unseen thing visible. In life, the view is always changing, but what we make remains. Or someone else comes along and marks over it, reacts to it, blows it up to make a dam, or erases it, prays on it, photographs it, or pays to see it. Each viewer brings something to or takes something from the image.

Petroglyphs shift like this face. They are part drawing, part sculpture, part of the whole of where they were placed, meant to be seen in this context, meant to make us look around or look inside or go somewhere or learn some fact. Or maybe not meant for us humans at all, perhaps meant to be treated in a very specific ceremonial manner. Certainly meant to be honored.

PUBLIC SITES

Asterisk denotes a site discussed or illustrated in the previous section.

There are about 150 rock art sites along the Northwest Coast, from Alaska to California. Most are located along the boulders on the beach or on rock outcroppings above the beach. Only a few sites are public parks.

BRITISH COLUMBIA (Canada)

Cape Mudge*
Drawings incised into beach boulders at Cape Mudge on Quadra Island north of Nanaimo, Vancouver Island.

Harewood Plain, Nanaimo*
Petroglyphs on 5 acres of bedrock. They are located about 2 miles southwest of Petroglyph Park at Nanaimo.

Monsell Petroglyph Site*
Thousand-year old images on a horizontal rock outcropping near Cedar, 5 miles south of Nanaimo City on the west bank of the Nanaimo River on Wilkerson Road. Uncovered in 1969, this is a private site owned by the Monsells.

Petroglyph Provincial Park*
Rock drawings located 2 miles south of Nanaimo, Vancouver Island, on Island Highway. Look for the "hogback" ridge across the harbour near Chase River.

Nanaimo Centennial Museum and Archives*
You can see the relocated Jack Point petroglyphs in Nanaimo installed in front of the museum at 100 Cameron Road.

Port Neville*
Many rock drawings can be viewed at low tide from the beach at Port Neville in an inlet known as Robber's Knob in Johnstone Strait.

Prince Rupert Harbour*
Life-sized intaglio carving called "man-who-fell-from-the-sky" plus other petroglyphs visible from the beach at low tides. The sites are located near Prince Rupert Harbour in northern British Columbia.

Sproat Lake, Vancouver Island*
Petroglyphs can be viewed at low tide during summer and fall from a platform in the lake.

Ringbolt Island*
Located in Kitselas Canyon on the Skeena River, these petroglyphs can only be viewed by boat when the water is low. Contact the Kitselas Band on Ringbolt Island for permission to visit.

QUEBEC

Qajartalik Island
Inuit rock carvings on Qajartalik Island near Wakeham Bay.

SASKATCHEWAN (Canada)

Indian Rock Art
Many red pictographs visible only by boat in the Churchill River system, including sites near Pelican Narrows, Larocque Lake, and Medicine Rapids.

Mistusinne Stone
A relocated stone sacred to the Cree, now about 2 kilometers southwest of the junction of Highway 19 and Road 749 near Elbow.

WASHINGTON

Cape Avala
Many drawings visible from the beach at Wedding Rocks. From Ozette Lake, follow a 3-mile trail to the beach, then a mile south to Wedding Rocks.

ACKNOWLEDGMENTS

I dedicate this book to Roger Mignon, my fellow artist and spouse. His eye is sharp; we still argue about the bird petroglyph I spotted on the canyon across from our place. He has his doubts! I appreciate the use of his photographs as the source for many of my drawings. His photos let me see the images twice.

Many friends have helped me through the lean period of writing this book—Sydney Hamburger, Sylvia Sleigh, Ora Lerman. They are all artists. To Ora, who listened to my discussions about this book from her hospital bed and offered her cogent insights, I address my unreachable greetings. To Lucy Lippard, writer and fellow activist, thank you for the loan of your petroglyph books and for your advice to "write what you know." You helped me keep focused. Laurie Tumer kindly read parts of the manuscript and used her teacher's eye to balance her comments against her photographer's insight. Artist Marina Gutiérrez was an early reader who shared my commitment to expand our art discourse beyond Western painting. Designer Larissa Lawrynenko suggested I draw petroglyphs for an earlier book on Native American history. Her gentle and warm response to those drawings encouraged me in this book. And thank you to my mother, Christine Parks Moore. Her pride in her father's Indian ancestry awakened my desire to educate myself about Native American cultures and to incorporate that awareness into my art and life.

I appreciate the hard work of the staff at Clear Light Publishers. Sara Held is an editor whose verbal skill is heightened by her wry humanity. Vicki Elliott, typographer, made the type design clear against the drawings. Marcia Keegan and Harmon Houghton believed that the drawings could make a book and supported me by their enthusiasm. And greetings across time to the many creators of the rock drawings. Their work is the true source of this book.

BIBLIOGRAPHY

Boas, Franz. *Primitive Art*. New York: Dover Publications, 1955.

Bray, Martha Coleman, and Edwin C. Bray, eds. and trans. *Joseph Nicollet on the Plains and Prairies: The Expeditions of 1838–1839, with Journals, Letters and Notes on Dakota Indians*. St. Paul: Minnesota Historical Press, 1976.

Brody, J. J. *Anasazi and Pueblo Painting*. A School of American Research Book. Albuquerque: University of New Mexico Press, 1991.

_____. *Mimbres Painted Pottery*. School of American Research. Albuquerque: University of New Mexico Press, 1977.

Brose, David S., James A. Brown, and David W. Penny. *Ancient Art of the American Woodland Indians*. New York: Harry N. Abrams, Inc. in association with Detroit Institute of Arts, 1985.

Campbell, Joseph. "Historical Atlas of World Mythology." vol. 2, *The Way of the Seeded Earth;* "Part 2: Mythologies of the Primitive Planters: The Northern Americas." New York: Harper & Row, 1989.

Cassidy, James J., ed. *Through Indian Eyes*. Pleasantville, N.Y./Montreal: Readers Digest, 1995.

Catlin, George. *Letters and Notes on the Manners, Customs and Conditions of North American Indians*, vols. 1 and 2. New York: Dover Publications, 1973.

Clark, Ella E. *Indian Legends of the Northern Rockies*. Norman: University of Oklahoma Press, 1996.

Cole, Sally J. *Legacy on Stone*. Boulder: Johnson Books, 1990.

Conway, Thor. *Painted Dreams: Native American Rock Art*. Minocqua, Wisc.: North Word Press, Inc., 1993.

Conway, Thor, and Julie Conway. *Spirits on Stone: The Agawa Pictographs*. San Luis Obispo, Calif.: Heritage Discoveries Publication #1, 1990.

Covarrubias, Miguel. *The Eagle, The Jaguar, and the Serpent: Indian Art of the Americas*. New York: Alfred A. Knopf, 1954.

Day, Jane S., Paul D. Friedman, and Marcia J. Tate, eds. "Rock Art of the Western Canyons," *Colorado Archaeological Society Memoir no. 3*. The Denver Museum of Natural History and the Colorado Archaeological Society, 1989.

de la Vega, Garcilaso. *The Florida of the Inca*. Translated and edited by John Grier Varner and Jeannette Jonson Varner. Austin: University of Texas Press, 1980.

Dixon, E. James. *Quest for the Origins of the First Americans*. Albuquerque: University of New Mexico Press, 1993.

Durham, Michael S. *Guide to Ancient Native American Sites*. Old Saybrook, Conn.: The Globe Pequot Press, 1994.

Erdoes, Richard, and Alfonso Ortiz. *American Indian Myths and Legends*. New York: Pantheon Books, 1984.

Fagan, Brian M. *Ancient North America: The Archaeology of a Continent*. London: Thames and Hudson, Ltd., 1991.

Fane, Diana, Ira Jacknis, and Lise M. Breen. *Objects of Myth and Memory: American Indian Art at the Brooklyn Museum*. Seattle: The Brooklyn Museum University of Washington Press, 1991.

Fewkes, Jesse Walter. *Hopi Kachinas*. New York: Dover Publications, 1985.

Fitzhugh, William W., and Aron Crowell. *Crossroads of Continents: Cultures of Siberia and Alaska*. Washington, D.C.: Smithsonian Institution Press, 1988.

Folsom, Franklin, and Mary Elting Folsom. *America's Ancient Treasures*. Albuquerque: University of New Mexico Press, 1993.

Garfield, Viola E., and Linn A. Forrest. *The Wolf and the Raven: Totem, Poles in Southeastern Alaska*. Seattle: University of Washington Press, 1992.

Grant, Campbell. *Rock Art of the American Indian*. Golden, Colo.: Outbooks, 1967.

Grant, Campbell, James W. Baird, and Kenneth J. Pringle. *Rock Drawings of the Coso Range*. China Lake, Calif.: Maturango Press, 1968.

Grinnell, George Bird. *The Cheyenne: Their History and Ways of Life*. New Haven, Conn.: Yale University Press, 1923.

Hadingham, Evan. *Early Man and the Cosmos*. Norman, Okla.: University of Oklahoma Press, 1985.

Hail, Barbara A., and Kate C. Duncan. *Out of the North: The Subarctic Collection of the Haffenreffer Museum of Anthropology*. Bristol, RI: Brown University, 1989.

Hill, Beth. *Guide to Indian Rock Carvings of the Pacific Northwest*. Blaine, Wash.: Hancock House Publishers, 1975.

Hill, Beth, and Ray Hill. *Indian Petroglyphs of the Pacific Northwest*. Seattle: University of Washington Press, 1978.

Hoffman, Walter J. "The Midewiwin or 'Grand Medicine Society' of the Ojibwa." *Seventh Annual Report of the Bureau of Ethnology for 1885–86*, 149-304. Washington, D.C.: Smithsonian Institution, 1891.

Hungry Wolf, Beverly. *The Ways of My Grandmothers*. New York: Quill, 1982.

Jonaitis, Aldona. *From the Land of the Totem Poles: The Northwest Coast Indian Art Collection at the American Museum of Natural History*. Seattle: University of Washington, 1991.

Kellar, Kenneth C., and Phyllis H. Keller. *Lines of Time*. Aberdeen, S.D.: North Plains Press, 1978.

Keyser, James D. *Indian Rock Art of the Columbia Plateau*. Seattle: University of Washington Press, and Vancouver/Toronto: Douglas & McIntyre, 1992.

Kilgo, Dolores A. *Likeness and Landscape: Thomas M. Easterly and the Art of the Daguerreotype.* Saint Louis: Missouri Historical Society, 1994.

Knaak, Manfred. *The Forgotten Artist: Indians of Anza-Borrego and Their Rock Art.* Borrego Springs, Calif.: Anza-Borrego Desert Natural History Association, 1988.

Leechman, D. "The Nanaimo Petroglyph," *Canadian Geographical Journal* 44.

Lowie, Robert H. "Shoshonean Tales," Journal of American Folklore 37: 1-242.

Mallery, Garrick. *Picture-Writing of the American Indians,* vols. 1 and 2. New York: Dover Publications, 1972.

Maurer, Evan M. *Visions of the People: A Pictorial History of Plains Indian Life.* Minneapolis: The Minneapolis Institute of Arts, 1992.

McCreery, Patricia, and Ekkehart Malotki. *Tapamveni: The Rock Art Galleries of Petrified Forest and Beyond.* Petrified Forest, Ariz.: Petrified Forest Museum Association, 1994.

McGlone, Bill, Ted Barker, and Phil Leonard. *Petroglyphs of Southeast Colorado and the Oklahoma Panhandle.* Kamas, Utah: Mithras, Inc., 1994.

McIlwraith, T. F. *The Bella Coola Indians.* Toronto: University of Toronto Press, 1948.

Meade, Edward. *Indian Rock Carvings of the Pacific Northwest.* Sidney, B.C: Gray's Publishing Ltd., 1971.

Nabokov, Peter, and Robert Easton. *Native American Architecture.* New York and London: Oxford University Press, 1989.

Nabokov, Peter. *Native American Testimony: A Chronicle of Indian-White Relations from Prophecy to Present.* New York: Viking Penguin, 1992.

Ortiz, Alfonso. *The Tewa World: Space, Time, Being and Becoming in a Pueblo Society.* Chicago: The University of Chicago Press, 1969.

Parker, Arthur C. *Parker on the Iroquois,* edited by William N. Fenton. Syracuse: Syracuse University Press, 1981.

Patterson, Alex. *A Field Guide to Rock Art Symbols of the Greater Southwest.* Boulder, Colo.: Johnson Books, 1992.

Pavesic, Max G., and William Studebaker. *Backtracking: Ancient Art of Southern Idaho.* Pocatello, Idaho: Idaho Museum of Natural History, 1993.

Penny, David W. *Art of the Ameircan Indian Frontier: The Chandler-Pohrt Collection.* Seattle: The Detroit Institute of Arts and University of Washington Press, 1992.

Phillips, Philip, and James A. Brown. *Pre-Columbian Shell Engravings From the Craig Mound at Spiro, Oklahoma.* Cambridge: Peabody Museum Press, Peabody Museum of Archaeology and Ethnology, Harvard University, 1978.

Preston, Robert A., and Ann L. Preston. "The Discovery of Nineteen Prehistoric Calendric Petroglyph Sites in Arizona," 123-133. *Earth and Sky,* ed. A. Benson and T. Hoskinson. Thousand Oaks, Calif.: Sl'ow Press, 1985.

Schaafsma, Polly. *Indian Rock Art of the Southwest.* Albuquerque: School of American Indian Research, University of New Mexico Press, 1980.

_____. *Rock Art in the Cochiti Reservoir District.* Papers in Anthropology no. 16. Santa Fe: Museum of New Mexico Press, 1967.

_____. *Rock Art in the Navaho Reservoir District.* Papers in Anthropology no. 7. Santa Fe: Museum of New Mexico Press, 1963.

Shafer, Harry J. *Ancient Texans: Rock Art & Lifeways Along the Lower Pecos.* Austin: Texas Monthly Press, published for the Witte Museum of the San Antonio Museum Association, 1986.

Skinner, Alanson. "Societies of the Iowa, Kansa and Ponca Indians," *Anthropological Paper of The American Museum of Natural History* II, 1915.

Speck, Frank, and Leonard Broom. *Cherokee Dance and Drama.* Norman and London: University of Oklahoma Press, 1983.

Steward, Julian H. *Petroglyphs of the United States,* extract from Smithsonian Institute Report, 1936. Seattle: The Shorey Book Store, 1972.

Taylor, Colin F. Editorial Consultant, and William C. Sturtevant, Technical Consultant. *The Native Americans: The Indigenous People of North America.* New York: Salamander Books, Ltd. and Smithmark Publishers, Inc., 1991.

Teit, James, A. "The Salishan Tribes of the Western Plateaus," edited by Franz Boas. Extract from 45th Annual Report of the Bureau of American Ethnology to the Smithsonian Institution, Washington D.C., 1930.

Trenton, Patricia, and Patrick T. Houlihan. *Native Americans: Five Centuries of Changing Images.* New York: Harry N. Abrams, 1989.

Utley, Robert M. *The Indian Frontier of the American West 1846–1890.* Albuquerque: The University of New Mexico Press, 1984.

Waldman, Carl. *Who Was Who in Native American History.* New York: Facts on File, 1990.

Waters, Frank. *Book of the Hopi.* New York: Viking Press, 1963.

Weigle, Marta, and Peter White. *The Lore of New Mexico.* Albuquerque: University of New Mexico Press, 1988.

Williamson, Ray A., and Claire R. Farrer, eds. *Earth and Sky: Visions of the Cosmos in Native American Folklore.* Albuquerque: University of New Mexico Press, 1992.

Wissler, Clark. "Societies and Ceremonial Associations in the Oglala Division of the Teton-Dakota," *Anthropological Papers of the American Museum of Natural History,* vol. II, 1-97, 1912.

Wyatt, Victoria. *Images from the Inside Passage: An Alaskan Portrait by Winter and Pond.* Seattle and London: University of Washington Press, in association with the Alaska State Library, 1989.

Young, M. Jane. *Signs From the Ancestors: Zuni Cultural Symbolism and Perceptions of Rock Art.* Albuquerque: University of New Mexico Press, 1988.

INDEX

Page references in **boldface type** refer to drawings.

Mogollon culture, 19, 24
Monsell Petroglyph Site (British Columbia), 168
Monster Slayer (War Twin), 33
Montana, public sites, 112–113
Moon (female deity), 46
moose, **118**, 119, **120**, **121**
Morning Star (Venus), 27
Mother of the Animals, 10
Mound Builders, 71, 76, 84
Mounds State Park (Indiana), 134
Moundville Archaeological Park (Alabama), 86
Mountain Lion, **34**, **35**, 106, **107**
Museum of Natural History (New York), 7
Myeengun ("Wolf"), 127

Nanaimo Centennial Museum and Archives (British Columbia), 149, 168
Nanaimo Petroglyph Park (Vancouver Island), frontispiece, 140, 145, 149, 154
Natchez people, 72
Navajo National Monument (Arizona), 41
Navajo people, 33
Nevada, public sites, 68–69
New Jersey, public sites, 135
New Mexico, public sites, 41–42
New York, public sites, 135
Newcombe, C. F., 140
Newspaper Rock Petroglyphs (Arizona), 41, 52
Newspaper Rock State Park (Utah), 69
Nicollet, John, 110
Nine-Mile Canyon Rock Art (Utah), 43
Nootka people, 149, 159
North Carolina, public sites, 87
North Dakota, public sites, 113
North Star, as Sky Coyote, 46
Northwest Coast, 136–168

peoples of, 138
Nova Scotia, public sites, 135

Ohio, public sites, 135
Ojibwa Anishinabe Nation, 124
Ojibwa Boulder Mosaic (Manitoba).
    See Bannock Point Petroform Site
Ojibwa people
    birch bark scrolls, 6
    pictographs, 119
    rock art sites, 115, 132
    supernaturals, 127
Oklahoma, public sites, 87
Ontario (Canada), public sites, 135
Oregon, public sites, 69
origin stories. *See* creation stories
Ortiz, Alfonso, 34
Otowi village (New Mexico), 10
Ozette (Washington), 138

Paalölöqangw (Hopi water serpent), 21
Painted Cave (Santa Barbara), 46
Painted Rocks State Park (Arizona), 41
Panther Cave (Texas), 113
Panther Intaglio (Wisconsin), 135
panthers, **34**, **35**, 106, **107**, 124, **126**, 127, **128**, **129**
    underwater, 78, **80**, 124, **126**, 127, **128**, **129**
Parowan Gap Indian Drawings (Utah), 43
Pavesic, Max G., 98
Peñasco Blanco (Chaco Canyon), 28
Penny, David W., 110, 131
Petrified Forest National Park (Arizona), 28, 35, 40, 41
petroglyph, defined, 1, 6
Petroglyph Canyon (Oregon), 59
Petroglyph National Monument (New Mexico), 28, 42